Operation IRAQI FREEDOM Key Decisions
Monograph Series

DECISIONMAKING IN OPERATION IRAQI FREEDOM: THE STRATEGIC SHIFT OF 2007

Steven Metz

John R. Martin
Executive Editor

May 2010

*****

Published by Books Express Publishing
Books Express, 2011
ISBN 978-1-780395-20-3

Books Express publications are available from all good retail and online booksellers. For
publishing proposals and direct ordering please contact us at: info@books-express.com

*****

This monograph is the second in a series that discusses decisionmaking during the conduct of Operation IRAQI FREEDOM. The previous volume is:

1. *Decisionmaking in Operation IRAQI FREEDOM: Removing Saddam Hussein by Force,* by Dr. Steven Metz, March 2010.

FOREWORD

In Volume 1 of the Operation IRAQI FREEDOM Key Decisions Monograph Series, Dr. Steven Metz skillfully studied the 2003 decision to go to war in Iraq. The results of that decision are widely called disastrous. In this second volume of the series, Dr. Metz looks carefully at the 2007 decision to surge forces into Iraq, a choice which is generally considered to have been effective in turning the tide of the war from potential disaster to possible—perhaps probable—strategic success. Although numerous strategic decisions remain to be made as the U.S. military executes its "responsible withdrawal" from Iraq, Dr. Metz has encapsulated much of the entire war in these two monographs, describing both the start and what may eventually be seen as the beginning of the end of the war. In this volume, he provides readers with an explanation of how a decision process that was fundamentally unchanged—with essentially the same people shaping and making the decision—could produce such a different result in 2007. As the current administration tries to replicate the surge in Afghanistan, this monograph is especially timely and shows the perils of attempting to achieve success in one strategic situation by copying actions successfully taken in another where different conditions applied.

Subsequent volumes of this series will analyze intervening and subsequent decisions, but Dr. Metz's two works have set a high standard for the succeeding monographs. I look forward to the needed debate that this volume and the others will generate.

DOUGLAS C. LOVELACE, Jr.
Director
Strategic Studies Institute

iv

PREFACE

Victory is still an option in Iraq.
Dr. Frederick Kagan[1]

The Strategic Shift of 2007.

By the time Fred Kagan penned the comment cited above, victory had already long been the wrong word to describe whatever outcome was going to befall the American adventure in Iraq. An argument can be made that victory — success against military foes in war — was an appropriate term in April 2003, when U.S. military forces deposed Saddam Hussein, but a military-only victory was far out of reach by 2007. The goal of victory articulated by Kagan and President George W. Bush perhaps still had merit in galvanizing public support of the war.[2] However, the better goal — particularly by late 2006, when a virulent insurgency and sectarian violence were raging in Iraq's cities — was some semblance of strategic success, which would not come about purely by military action. That success would necessarily include a significant military component, but also required a broader approach that would support Iraq's economic, political, and societal development. Just as victory over Adolf Hitler in World War II required the Marshall Plan to cement the achievements of combat in Europe, the "victory" of 2003 in Iraq would require by 2007 much more than just military force to produce conditions that would ultimately be helpful to advancing American interests in the Middle East.

The military component of the 2007 effort to achieve a positive result in Iraq became popularly known as "the surge." In this second volume of the Strategic

Studies Institute's Operation IRAQI FREEDOM Key Decisions Monograph Series, Dr. Steven Metz covers this critical decision in the Iraq war, but correctly posits that the surge was only part of a broad strategic shift that produced the success — still tenuous — of 2008 and beyond. In doing so, Dr. Metz debunks some of the "surge triumphalism." In this view, the surge was almost solely responsible for the improvements in security that enabled the emerging positive results in Iraq. General David Petraeus — the man whose name became synonymous with the surge — sees it differently. General Petraeus, who led the surge of troops into Iraq in 2007, freely admits that the success of the surge was due to a confluence of factors. Those factors include Iraqis tiring of both Sunni and Shi'a extremists, Iraqi Security Forces achieving at least limited capacity to provide security, and the U.S. military's growth in tactical and operational prowess in counterinsurgency. Dr. Metz argues that a "perfect storm" of conditions, accompanied by "good thinking, good luck, and good timing," were what allowed the success of the strategic shift that he describes. Dr. Metz may give short shrift to President George W. Bush's resolve and to the skill that General Petraeus and other senior leaders brought to the surge — or the strategic shift — but he presents a solid case against using the surge as a model for future operations, including in Afghanistan. Without similar conditions — and good thinking, luck, and timing — the surge of troops in Afghanistan may not produce anything like the positive strategic results that appear to be emerging in Iraq.

There are no easy fixes to the challenges identified by Dr. Metz, but his recommendations include:

- **Be skeptical of basing force development and military strategy on the 2007-08 experience in**

Iraq. Preparing to fight the last war may be the comfortable thing to do, but the situation will change and the enemy will adapt. Basing strategy and force development solely on how effectively the Army fought the counterinsurgency in Iraq is folly. At the same time, neglecting the lessons learned from Iraq would also be foolish.

• **Use Army intellectual resources to lead a basic reconceptualization of the way the U.S. Government and American political leaders think about insurgency and counterinsurgency.** Uniformed military leaders may have the right strategic thinking about insurgency and counterinsurgency. However, if their political leaders do not share that understanding—or refuse to accept military advice—future efforts at supporting allies in counterinsurgency efforts will be long and costly and may not produce desired results.

• **Increase attention to strategic communication skills in leader selection and development programs.** The development of military strategic leaders is an arcane art form, not a science. One of the talents needed in those leaders is the ability to communicate to broad audiences: to an indigenous population in the theater of operations, to international players providing support or coalition members, to the U.S. domestic audience. Even all these years after the Vietnam War, the U.S. military—especially at some of the most-senior levels—still remains wary of engagement with the media, which is essential for the strategic communication tasks. Although development of these skills will undoubtedly remain a challenge for years to come, the task of identifying them in strategic leaders should not be so difficult. The ability to communicate on the strategic level must be considered when promoting general officers into the highest ranks.

- **Develop a rapidly-deployable surge capacity for creating, training, and equipping local security forces.** The recently-concluded *Quadrennial Defense Review* does not appear to include guidance to develop a separate force for this purpose, although it does suggest strengthening the ability of general purpose forces to do so.[3]

- **Maintain the Army's wartime adaptation speed.** This recommendation should probably extend to the entire military, not just the Army, but the Army and the Marine Corps are the most-heavily engaged forces in Iraq and are probably adapting more rapidly than the other Services. Wartime acts as a catalyst for adaptation, so it may be unrealistic to expect that same speed to be maintained whenever the military finally encounters a peacetime situation.

- **Lead an effort within the joint community to develop and institutionalize procedures for reseizing the strategic initiative.** Future conflicts — like Iraq — may see the United States lose the strategic initiative. It only makes sense now to prepare in education and exercises for that eventuality.

One final recommendation from Dr. Metz is included in the body of his report: he recommends that Congress consider formal establishment of a strategic council comprised of the Service chiefs and the combatant commanders. Strategic advice that comes from this council should represent both the needs of any conflict—provided by the combatant commanders—and the requirements for the long-term health of the individual Services—more likely to originate with the Service chiefs. Advice to the President and to the Secretary of Defense should cover both perspectives.

The Key Decisions Series.[4]

The first and second volumes of the Strategic Studies Institute's Operation IRAQI FREEDOM Key Decisions Monograph Series act as bookends for the series. The first covered the decision to go to war in Iraq, while this volume covers the decision that may ultimately be seen as leading to the end of the war. While one of the volumes (challenges of withdrawing from Iraq) will cover events that happened after the surge, all the other decisions happened within the time frame of the decision to go to war in 2003 and the decision to surge forces in 2007.

Authors in this series are asked to concentrate on the decisions more than on the subsequent effects. The effort should focus on identifying the factors that influenced the decision—either positively or negatively—and determining whether the factors were idiosyncratic or systemic in nature. That determination is key in devising solutions to problems or to reinforcing positive factors. Authors should answer six questions about their analyzed decision:

1. Who were the key decision makers?
2. Who shaped or influenced the decision?
3. What was the political and strategic context of the decision?

4. What options were considered?

5. What decisionmaking and analysis process was used?

6. What criteria were used to make the decision?

While the Strategic Studies Institute is willing to consider proposals for studies evaluating other key decisions, those already selected for analysis are:[5]

1. The decision in 2003 to go to war. (Status: complete.[6])

2. The decision in 2002 and 2003 to plan for a war of liberation, minimum reconstruction, and rapid turn-over to an Iraqi government. (Status: an author has been identified.)

3. The decision in 2003 to occupy the country rather than quickly returning sovereignty to Iraqis. (Status: an author has been identified.)

4. The decision in 2004 to focus on development of the Iraqi Security Forces. (Status: an author has been identified.)

5. The decision in 2004 and beyond to follow a strategy of transitioning the security responsibilities to the Iraqi government. (Status: the Strategic Studies Institute is still seeking an author.)

6. The decision in 2007 to "surge" forces into Iraq as part of a strategic shift. (Status: complete with this publication.)

7. The various decisions that made the fight "more interagency." (Status: an author has been identified.)

8. The various decisions that affected the establishment and functioning of the government of Iraq. (Status: the Strategic Studies Institute is still seeking an author.)

9. The various decisions that affect the responsible drawdown of forces in 2009 and beyond. (Status: the Strategic Studies Institute is still seeking an author.)

*****

While the decision to surge troops into Iraq in 2007 is widely seen as a good choice, it still requires the careful examination that Dr. Metz brings to all his work. Without such meticulous study, the wise decision in a particular theater at a certain point in time may be misconstrued to be a solid solution for other theaters where very different conditions exist. The Strategic Studies Institute hopes that study of the good decision—at least as judged by the emerging results—to surge troops into Iraq in 2007 will generate just as much debate as study of the many poor ones made in this particular war. Better understanding—of both good and bad decisions—should lead to better choices in future operating environments.

JOHN R. MARTIN
Executive Editor
OIF Key Decisions Project
Strategic Studies Institute

ENDNOTES - PREFACE

1. Frederick W. Kagan, "Choosing Victory: A Plan for Success in Iraq," Phase I report of the Iraq Planning Group at the American Enterprise Institute, January 25, 2007, p. 1.

2. President Bush used the rhetoric of victory many times, doing so officially in *National Strategy for Victory in Iraq*, Washington, DC: National Security Council, November 2005.

3. "Quadrennial Defense Review Report," Washington, DC: U.S. Department of Defense, February 2010, p. 29.

4. A fuller explication of the OIF Key Decisions Monograph Series can be found in the preface to the first volume of the series. See Steven Metz, *Decisionmaking in Operation Iraqi Freedom: Removing Saddam Hussein By Force*, OIF Key Decisions Monograph Series, Vol. 1, Colonel (Retired) John R. Martin, Executive ed., Carlisle, PA: Strategic Studies Institute, U.S. Army War College, February 2010, pp. v-xvii.

5. Procedures for submitting unsolicited manuscripts are found at the SSI website, available from *www.strategicstudiesinstitute. army.mil*. Submissions for this series should be directed to SSI's Director of Research, who will provide them to the series executive editor.

6. This decision was studied in the first volume of this series. See Metz.

ABOUT THE CONTRIBUTORS

STEVEN METZ is Chairman of the Regional Strategy Department and Research Professor of National Security Affairs at the Strategic Studies Institute (SSI). He has been with SSI since 1993, previously serving as Henry L. Stimson Professor of Military Studies and SSI's Director of Research. Dr. Metz has also been on the faculty of the Air War College, the U.S. Army Command and General Staff College, and several universities. He has been an advisor to political campaigns and elements of the intelligence community; served on national security policy task forces; testified in both houses of Congress; and spoken on military and security issues around the world. He is the author of more than 100 publications, including articles in journals such as *Washington Quarterly*, *Joint Force Quarterly*, *The National Interest*, *Defence Studies*, and *Current History*. Dr. Metz's research has taken him to 30 countries, including Iraq immediately after the collapse of the Hussein regime. He currently serves on the RAND Corporation's Insurgency Board. He is the author of *Iraq and the Evolution of American Strategy* and is working on a book entitled *Strategic Shock: Eight Events That Changed American Security*. Dr. Metz holds a Ph.D. from the Johns Hopkins University.

JOHN R. MARTIN joined SSI in mid-2009 and is the Institute's specialist in joint, interagency, intergovernmental, and multinational issues. Professor Martin previously served at SSI from 2000 to 2004, serving as the Chairman of the Art of War Department and concurrently as the Institute's Deputy Director. Professor Martin was also a visiting professor at SSI in 2006 and 2007. Professor Martin served in the

U.S. Army for over 31 years, retiring as a colonel. He served extensively in the Republic of Korea, primarily in tactical Aviation, but also with the United Nations Command Military Armistice Commission and as commander of a liaison team with the Republic of Korea Army. He also possesses considerable experience in Washington, DC, where he worked on Army force structure, manning the force, the RAH-66 Comanche helicopter program, and providing language training. While in the Army, Professor Martin was operationally deployed to Guam (1975: Operation NEW LIFE), Kosovo (1999: Task Force Falcon), Bosnia (1999-2000: SFOR), Afghanistan (2002: CJTF-180) and Iraq (2003: ORHA/CPA; 2005: MNSTC-I; 2007: MNF-I). Professor Martin was the Executive Editor of *Hard Lessons: The Iraq Reconstruction Experience*. This major government report by the Special Inspector General for Iraq Reconstruction was published in early 2009 and analyzed the reconstruction of Iraq since 2003. Professor Martin graduated with highest distinction from the College of Naval Command and Staff at the Naval War College, Newport, RI, in 1988. He is a 1996 graduate of the National War College and holds Master's Degrees in National Security Affairs from both institutions. Professor Martin also holds a Master's Degree in Aeronautical Engineering from the U.S. Naval Postgraduate School and is a graduate of the U.S. Naval Test Pilot School at Patuxent River, MD. He is a 1974 graduate of the U.S. Military Academy at West Point, NY.

DECISIONMAKING IN OPERATION IRAQI FREEDOM: THE STRATEGIC SHIFT OF 2007

> As to whether the United States has made mistakes, of course, I'm sure, we have. You can't be involved in something as big as the liberation of a country like Iraq and all that has happened since, and I'm sure there are things that we could have done differently. . . .
>
> Secretary of State Condoleezza Rice[1]

INTRODUCTION

When the Bush administration elected to invade Iraq in 2003 to remove Saddam Hussein from power, no senior policymaker anticipated that there would be extensive and protracted armed resistance after the dictator was gone.[2] The administration assumed that the Iraqi bureaucracy and security forces—both military and police—would return to work once they had new leadership untainted by association with Hussein. But American policymakers did not understand how fragile and precarious Iraq was after decades of pathological rule. As Iraqi security forces disappeared, the nation collapsed into a spasm of looting and street crime. All administration and public order collapsed. It was "Lord of the Flies" on a monumental scale. Anarchy sparked public anger which gathered energy with each passing week. Personal and sectarian hostility, which had been suppressed by Hussein, raged unfettered. Revenge haunted the streets—and it was armed. For a brief interlude, little violence was directed against Americans. But that did not last long.

1

Trouble first exploded in the restive city of Fallujah, 35 miles west of Baghdad. The U.S. military had bypassed the city in its assault on Baghdad, but elements of the 82d Airborne Division arrived in late April. Fallujah did not take kindly to occupation, and the 82d did not take kindly to occupation duty. Within a few days, a rally celebrating Saddam Hussein's birthday led to angry denunciations of the U.S. presence and heated demands for withdrawal. Shooting broke out, leaving at least 13 Iraqis dead.[3] Two more died the next day in a second round of clashes. Attackers then tossed grenades into a U.S. Army compound.

In early May, two American Soldiers were killed in Baghdad. A few weeks later, two more died during a nighttime attack on an Army checkpoint near Fallujah. Violence spread to Baghdad and the region west and north of the capital known as the "Sunni triangle." The initial attacks were unsophisticated, but this soon changed as veteran soldiers unemployed by the disbanding of the Iraqi army joined in. Armed bands began to focus on isolated checkpoints and slow-moving convoys. They made greater use of rockets and mortars, allowing them to retreat and fight again rather than die *en masse* as the Saddam Fedayeen irregulars had in the March and April battles. Iraqis who worked for the Americans or were part of the new government and administrative structure became targets. Translators were among the favorites. Insurgents sabotaged the electrical grid, water system, and oil pipelines. Like their forebears in earlier insurgencies, Iraqi fighters seemed to understand that a country's rulers—the Americans in this case—were blamed for the lack of water, electricity, and fuel even when the insurgents themselves were responsible. The greater public anger and frustration, the insurgents knew, the better for them.

Over the summer, a group of Hussein loyalists calling itself *al-Awda* ("the return") made open overtures to Islamic militants linked to al Qaeda. There were reports of former regime officials recruiting foreign fighters. U.S. forces soon encountered Syrians, Saudis, Yemenis, Algerians, Lebanese, and Chechens, indicating that the international jihadist network, born in Afghanistan in the 1980s, was refocusing on Iraq. Insurgent leaders began paying unemployed Iraqi men with military and police training and criminals released from prison earlier in the year to kill American troops.

As early as June, some strategic analysts warned that the fighting constituted an organized guerrilla war. But U.S. officials rejected this idea. Secretary of Defense Donald Rumsfeld attributed the violence to "the remnants of the Ba'ath regime and Fedayeen death squads" and "foreign terrorists" who were "being dealt with in an orderly and forceful fashion by coalition forces."[4] As summer wore on, though, it was increasingly difficult to sustain that position. Finally, on July 16, General John Abizaid, commander of the U.S. Central Command, admitted that the United States faced "a classical guerrilla type campaign." "It's low-intensity conflict in our doctrinal terms," he said, "but it's war, however you describe it."[5] The optimism of a month earlier, the hope of a quick and relatively painless transition to a post-Hussein Iraq, was shattered.

Initially the United States did not develop a comprehensive strategy for counterinsurgency support in Iraq, or a national strategy which explained the rationale for U.S. involvement and the ultimate political objectives.[6] These only took shape during 2004 and 2005 as the insurgency grew. The strategy stressed increasing the size and effectiveness of the Iraqi Security Forces (ISF) and turning over responsibility to them as quickly as possible. This reflected a long-standing truth of counterinsurgency support: outsiders can *influence* the outcome, but only locals can *determine* it. Ultimately the Iraqis themselves had to defeat the insurgents. In fact, some U.S. military and civilian leaders were convinced that American military forces provoked hostility among the Iraqi people, and thus sought to minimize the U.S. role, keeping American troops off the streets as much as possible and limiting their contact with the population.

This did not work. Creating a new ISF proved harder than expected. With few effective Iraqi security forces and not enough Americans to secure all of the country around the clock, the insurgency spread and mutated. Attacks became better coordinated and more sophisticated, particularly those using improvised explosive devices (IEDs) and vehicle borne improvised explosive devices (VBIED). Foreign extremists linked to al Qaeda, and under the leadership of the Jordanian Abu Musab al-Zarqawi, began targeting Iraqi Shiites. Nineteenth century Russian revolutionaries used to assert "the worse, the better," meaning that anything that eroded public order and trust in the government helped their cause. The Iraq insurgents put this into practice. Eventually Shiite militias began striking back. "By the summer of 2006," journalist Linda Robinson wrote, "Baghdad was on fire. Sectarian violence was spilling into all-out civil war, and it swept up hundreds of thousands of Iraqis."[7] The ISF, while improving, were overwhelmed and remained weak in key areas. Some units were simply dysfunctional. Others joined

4

the sectarian violence, serving the government by day and sectarian militias by night. By the end of 2006, the U.S. Department of Defense (DoD) grimly noted that, "Attack levels—both overall and in all specific measurable categories—were the highest on record during this reporting period. . . ."[8]

Then things began to turn. In January 2007, President George W. Bush announced a new approach in Iraq which increased the number of U.S. military forces, refocused them on population security, and redoubled reconstruction assistance and support to political reform. While the strategic shift experienced a rocky start—American casualties increased during the first half of 2007—Iraq eventually began to stabilize. By March 2009, the DoD reported that, "violence has dropped dramatically in the last 2 years, and normal life continues to return to the country."[9] Today attacks continue, but there is precarious stability. The U.S. military is no longer involved in combat operations and soon will have only a training and advisory force in Iraq. That country's future certainly remains unclear— renewed sectarian violence or a revived insurgency are possible. However, Iraq at least has an opportunity.

The popular perception is that the strategic shift of 2007, which is often simply called "the surge," snatched victory from imminent defeat. According to this thinking, the United States was implementing a flawed strategy but then had a burst of insight. As a result of the surge, "America won and al Qaeda, the Ba'athists, and the Iranians lost."[10] Reality is more complex. The strategy which had taken shape by 2005 was appropriate for that time, given both conditions in Iraq and the wider strategic context. During 2006, though, the essential nature of the conflict changed, thus requiring a strategic shift to allow the United

5

States and the Iraqi government to recapture the initiative. The strategic shift of 2007 succeeded through a combination of good thinking, good luck, and good timing. This monograph will explore the decisionmaking process that led to the strategic shift, drawing implications and recommendations for military involvement in strategy formulation.

THE DECISION

Political and Strategic Context.

Decisionmaking on national security is shaped not only by the particulars of a given issue, but also by the wider political and strategic context. During the Bush administration the "global war on terrorism" (GWOT) was the dominant contextual component or central organizing concept of American strategy. The Iraq conflict was understood and portrayed in relationship to this. The concern was not simply Iraq's *inherent* importance, but the *symbolism* of the conflict. The thinking was that America's adversaries and partners would draw conclusions about the United States from the outcome in Iraq and act accordingly. An American defeat would embolden adversaries and frighten partners. Victory would have the opposite effect.[11]

By 2006, the Bush administration defined Iraq as the "central front" in the GWOT.[12] "A failed Iraq," President Bush stated in August 2006, "would make America less secure. A failed Iraq in the heart of the Middle East will provide safe haven for terrorists and extremists. It will embolden those who are trying to thwart the ambitions of reformers. In this case, it would give the terrorists and extremists an additional tool besides safe haven, and that is revenue from oil sales."[13] Building on this, the Bush strategy in Iraq, like all strategies, reflected a series of assumptions:

- The conflict in Iraq was a component of the global struggle between Islamic "moderates" (defined as those friendly to the United States who sought democracy) and "extremists" pursuing Taliban-style theocracies, in essence a struggle between freedom and its enemies;[14]
- The objective of al Qaeda and its affiliates was the downfall of the United States;
- Al Qaeda and its affiliates were interested in Iraq as a sanctuary and resource for the next stage of their offensive against America. Hence, Iraq was important because al Qaeda considered it important.

Unintentionally, this perspective allowed al Qaeda to define the conflict in Iraq. The United States was compelled to undertake counterinsurgency support not because it wanted to, but because al Qaeda—America's arch-enemy—had instigated insurgency. The problem was that insurgency is a type of conflict that avoids America's strengths and exploits its weaknesses. Insurgency is, for instance, protracted and costly, often with ambiguous outcomes. Americans favor (and are good at) short conflicts with decisive results. Counterinsurgency lacks moral clarity since the regime which the United States supports is, by definition, deeply flawed. It may be corrupt, repressive, unrepresentative, fragmented, or simply ineffective. This makes it difficult to sustain the public and congressional support needed for long-term involvement. Because of this, Presidents committed to counterinsurgency support emphasize the strategic stakes, warning of the great costs and risks of defeat (and defining defeat as the failure to decisively defeat the insurgents). In Vietnam, the Johnson administration portrayed a communist victory as the beginning of communist control of all of Southeast Asia. In Iraq, the Bush administration stated that insurgent success would provide al Qaeda the type of victory that would make it a much more dangerous enemy. By portraying the stakes as expansive and dire, the United States becomes firmly committed to the regime facing an insurgency. While necessary from the perspective of domestic politics, this ties a President's hands. It diminishes his influence over the allied regime and "hardens" the issue, leaving little flexibility in defining or adjusting ultimate objectives.

That is precisely what happened in Iraq. To bolster support for American involvement in the conflict, the Bush administration portrayed a failure to do so as catastrophic, linking the survival of the Iraqi regime directly to American security. "The worst mistake would be," according to President Bush, "to think that if we pulled out, the terrorists would leave us alone. They will not leave us alone. They will follow us. The safety of America depends on the outcome of the battle in the streets of Baghdad."[15] The security of the American homeland, in other words, depended on the counterinsurgency campaign in Iraq. As the debate unfolded, this took any serious reconsideration of strategic *objectives* off the table. Only the ways and means of the strategy were open for discussion.

There was more opposition to the strategic shift of 2007 than any of the other key decisions that framed Operation IRAQI FREEDOM. Congressional resistance emerged early. In November 2005, the late Congressman John Murtha (D-PA), a veteran with a pro-military reputation, introduced House

Joint Resolution 73 calling for the withdrawal of American troops. Murtha, according to Peter Feaver, "was advocating the wholesale abandonment of Iraq."[16] A July 2006 letter to President Bush from 12 leading congressional Democrats asserted that "your Administration lacks a coherent strategy to stabilize Iraq and achieve victory" and "simply staying the course in Iraq is not working."[17] In 2006, the House of Representatives passed a nonbinding resolution calling for a withdrawal deadline. But congressional opposition was thwarted—at least temporarily—by President Bush's success in portraying the conflict as part of the struggle against al Qaeda, and in popularizing the notion that opposition to American involvement was tantamount to being opposed to the American forces fighting the war. But this simply bought time. Bush understood that Congress eventually would end U.S. involvement in Iraq if the conflict did not turn around. After all, it was Congress that had forced American disengagement from an earlier counterinsurgency campaign in Vietnam. There was, then, a closing window of opportunity.

Meanwhile, the public was bitterly divided. With the Internet, 24-hour cable news, and talk radio inflaming passions, Iraq became the most divisive partisan issue in modern American politics, surpassing even Vietnam.[18] With Iraq a major factor, President Bush's approval rating plummeted.[19] But as often happens, the President facing an unpopular war—Lincoln and the Civil War, Truman and Korea, Johnson and Vietnam—could not simply abandon it, whether out of concern for the wider damage to American prestige and security or with personal legacy. Like those earlier unpopular wars, the goal in Iraq became finding an attainable form of success even if it did not match the initial lofty goals. This interplay of strategy and politics reflected a deep tradition. Americans consistently blend strategy, public opinion, and electoral considerations. More than most other democracies, the United States considers national security a valid topic for partisanship. Politics and strategy are not simply linked—they are indistinguishable. Because the public has a role in shaping national security strategy but has a very shallow understanding of it, issues are simplified, painted in stark black and white. Information profusion adds to this, making nuance or compromise difficult, if not impossible. Political discourse and strategic debates often become a clash of opposing caricatures.

As the 2006 mid-term elections approached, Democrats recognized that Iraq was the greatest vulnerability of President Bush and, by default, Republicans in general, so they made it the centerpiece of their campaigns. Republican ("Grand Old Party" [GOP]) candidates were in a bind: President Bush—the leader of their party—had staked his reputation and his legacy on an increasingly unpopular conflict. "Senior Republican strategists said they told candidates to avoid talking about the war, and even to distance themselves from it, and urged the White House to change its approach, at least through November," the *New York Times* reported. "But that strategy was undercut by Mr. Bush and Mr. Dick Cheney, who kept making the case for victory in forum after forum, ensuring that the issue remained in public view."[20] That October 2006 was the deadliest month for American troops since 2004 made it even worse.

The November 2006 election led to a tremendous victory for the Democrats as they won control of both houses of Congress. The message was clear. As Senator

Edward M. Kennedy (D-MA) put it on election day, "Today is really a referendum on President Bush's handling of the war in Iraq."[21] Support was even weakening within the GOP. A month before the election Senator John W. Warner (R-VA), chairman of the Senate Armed Services Committee, said that the United States should consider a "change of course" if the violence in Iraq continued to escalate.[22] A few weeks after the election, Senator Chuck Hagel (R-NE) wrote that, "The United States must begin planning for a phased troop withdrawal from Iraq. The cost of combat in Iraq in terms of American lives, dollars and world standing has been devastating."[23] Even Secretary of Defense Donald Rumsfeld, in a November 6 memo later leaked to the press, admitted that "what U.S. forces are currently doing in Iraq is not working well enough or fast enough."[24]

In a post-election news conference, President Bush indicated his willingness to consider new options and work with the Democratic leadership in Congress, but again refused to contemplate withdrawal or set a date for it. He continued to portray the options in Iraq in stark terms, as victory or catastrophic defeat. Like Abraham Lincoln in the first 3 years of the Civil War, Bush was inflexible on broad strategic objectives but flexible on tactics, operational methods, force levels and, eventually, personnel. The day after the 2006 election, he announced that Secretary Rumsfeld, who had been the primary architect of American strategy in Iraq since the decision to remove Saddam Hussein by force, would be replaced by Robert Gates, former Director of the Central Intelligence Agency (CIA). President Bush also launched a sweeping formal review of Iraq policy across his administration to build on several informal reviews which were already underway.[25] The stage appeared set for a dramatic shift in America's Iraq strategy.

Mounting stress on the U.S. military, particularly the Army and Marine Corps, also influenced the decisionmaking. Like the decline in public and congressional support, this added to the notion that a clock was ticking, that the opportunity to turn things around in Iraq was fleeting. Pressure on the ground forces increased as soon as the insurgency emerged. Neither the Army nor the Marine Corps were configured for large scale, protracted counterinsurgency. A decade of defense transformation had created a force optimized for intense, short-duration operations, not stabilization or counterinsurgency.[26] The U.S. military was like a finely-trained sprinter suddenly entered in a marathon. In September 2003, the Congressional Budget Office (CBO) published a widely-discussed report that questioned the ability of the Army to sustain its rotation in Iraq after March 2004 without extending tours beyond 1 year.[27] Doing so could adversely affect recruitment and retention, potentially forcing service leaders to compromise on the quality of people who entered the military, and to spend additional funds keeping those they had. The CBO warning proved false—the Army did find a way to sustain its commitment. But the costs were real and seemed likely to mount as the insurgency dragged on.

Critics contended that at its existing size, the Army could not undertake protracted large-scale stabilization operations, continue transformation, perform its other worldwide missions, and sustain the quality of its troops, leaders, and equipment.[28] The only solution, they felt, was increasing the overall size of the American military, particularly the ground forces.[29] Congress, eager to demonstrate its seriousness in the war on terrorism, jumped on board.[30] Secretary Rumsfeld resisted, arguing that additional troops would draw resources from the ongoing defense transformation that he badly wanted. "The real problem," he wrote, "is not necessarily the size of our active and reserve military components, *per se*, but rather how forces have been managed, and the mix of capabilities at our disposal."[31]

In 2004, the Army again extended the tours of some units in Iraq, returned others more quickly than planned, and began exploring other unpleasant measures such as shorter leaves. At that time General Peter Schoomaker, the Army Chief of Staff, admitted that Iraq was "stressing" the Army but advised that he could support at least 3 more years at existing deployment levels without an overall force increase.[32] Trouble, though, lay ahead. "What keeps me awake at night," General Richard Cody, the Army Vice Chief of Staff, told Congress, "is what will this all-volunteer force look like in 2007."[33] The word "hollow," which was used to describe the weakened, post-Vietnam Army, reappeared.[34] By 2006 General Schoomaker grimly warned that the active duty Army "will break" under the strain of repeated rotations into Iraq and Afghanistan.[35] In 2007, Admiral Michael Mullen, the Chairman of the Joint Chiefs of Staff (JCS), expressed concern that deployments in Iraq and Afghanistan left the Army and Marine Corps unprepared for large scale conventional warfare.[36]

The final—and most important—contextual component framing the strategic shift of 2007 was the decaying security situation in Iraq itself.[37] Violence was endemic and paralyzing. Large parts of the country had minimal or no government control. The Iraqi security forces were expanding in size and effectiveness, but were still far from capable of securing the nation. There was no indication that this was about to change.

Decisionmakers.

Because President Bush saw the GWOT as the preeminent task of his administration and Iraq as its central battlefield, he made the key strategic decisions himself. This reflects the long-standing tradition of American Presidents: the more important an issue, the more they directly make key decisions. To the extent that President Bush delegated responsibility for Iraq strategy, the most influential officials were Secretary Rumsfeld; General John Abizaid, commander of the U.S. Central Command (CENTCOM); and General George Casey, commander of Multi-National Force-Iraq (MNF-I). President Bush consulted regularly with his field commanders, but the focus appears to have been on operational level questions rather than broad strategic issues. He did regularly ask them if the United States should be doing things differently in Iraq. But there is no record of the President consulting uniformed leaders on whether the counterinsurgency effort or the commitment to the Iraqi government was appropriate.

Bush's claims that he always deferred to military advice was not wholly accurate if the reports of journalists are correct. Bob Woodward, for instance, describes a "simmering private battle" between President Bush and General Casey that had emerged by 2006, stemming largely from the President's focus on insurgent casualties (which smacked of the "body count" mentality in Vietnam.)[38] By necessity, contact between the President and his military commanders was regular—particularly compared to those in the

Clinton administration—but not daily. With the exception of general officers who served as National Security Adviser (Brent Scowcroft and Colin Powell), it is always difficult for those in uniform to form and sustain a close personal relationship with the President.

The Process.

Until the second half of 2006, President Bush deferred to Rumsfeld's insistence that a rapid transition to Iraqi security forces and a shift of the American role to support and training was most viable. Bush set the broad, overarching objectives and then tasked others to find ways to attain them. The issue—and it is a persistent one in American strategy—was the extent of presidential involvement in strategy. Both micromanagement and detachment from strategy making by a President create problems. The key is finding the appropriate balance. Until 2006, though, President Bush leaned toward detachment and delegation. Bing West—never one to mince words—contends that, "Bush had recused himself from strategy as well as tactics. . . ."[39] The result was a dissonance between Secretary Rumsfeld's approach to Iraq and President Bush's stated objective which persisted for several years. This led to confusing strategic guidance for the military commanders. As journalists David Cloud and Greg Jaffe explain:

> Bush had told himself he would not micromanage his generals, the way Lyndon Johnson had done. Just as some parts of the Army had vowed never to refight Vietnam, so too had the president. But Bush took his own maxim to the extreme, leaving his commanders without any real instructions except for the advice they got from Rumsfeld. While the president was

insisting that the United States was in a life-or-death struggle to change the Middle East, Rumsfeld was essentially telling his top commander [Casey] that he shouldn't try too hard.[40]

This dissonance became starker as the security situation in Iraq eroded. Three major combined U.S.-Iraq operations to stabilize Baghdad in 2006— Operations SCALES OF JUSTICE, TOGETHER FORWARD, and TOGETHER FORWARD II—could not stem the violence.[41] When U.S. forces moved into a neighborhood, violence dropped, but always resumed when they moved out. The ISF were simply unable or unwilling to hold the cleared areas, much less build sustained security. It was clear by the summer of 2006 that the United States was not on track for victory as President Bush described it.

When the United States undertakes protracted counterinsurgency, stabilization, or peacekeeping operations, it must tailor its strategy both to attain national objectives and sustain support for the effort. The American public has a limited tolerance for U.S. casualties when it questions the importance of a conflict.[42] The problem for the Bush administration was that its primary rationale for involvement in Iraq—that al Qaeda had deemed it important, and that fighting extremists there meant that we did not have to fight them here—simply did not take full root outside the political right. To preserve the increasingly fragile public and congressional support for involvement, the Bush administration needed a strategy which would minimize American casualties. But this detracted from mission effectiveness. As historian Kimberly Kagan describes it:

In 2006, the overwhelming majority of American combat forces had been concentrated on FOBs (forward operating bases), from which they reinforced Iraqi Security Forces and conducted patrols in violent areas. U.S. military operations tended to be reactive rather than proactive, episodic rather than sustained. The insufficiently trained and equipped Iraqi Security Forces had been pushed prematurely into the fight. Rather than conducting counterinsurgency operations they often relied on ineffective checkpoints. As a result, security ebbed and flowed throughout neighborhoods and towns but was rarely lasting, and the presence of Coalition Forces provided little sense of security for Iraqi civilians.[43]

As always, American strategy unfolded in a politically-charged environment with what Carl von Clausewitz, the esteemed theorist of war, considered the "rational" dimension—using force to attain political ends—intermixed with the emotions of public opinion, much of it based on limited information and understanding.

History demonstrates that when an outside power undertakes counterinsurgency support, the effectiveness of the partner government rather than the strategy of the outsider is the ultimate determinant of success. But in Iraq, there were deep questions about the willingness and ability of the inexperienced Iraqi Prime Minister Nouri al-Maliki and his key advisers to control the sectarian violence which had, by 2006, surpassed the insurgency in intensity and destructiveness. General Casey and U.S. Ambassador Zalmay Khalilzad devoted extensive time to helping Maliki understand the role of a national leader in the face of an insurgency. But after a visit to Iraq, National Security Adviser Stephen Hadley noted that Maliki offered "reassuring words," but was either secretly empowering "an aggressive push to consolidate Shia power and influence" or was "ignorant of what was going on."[44] Testimony by Air Force General Michael Hayden, Director of the CIA, to the Iraq Study Group—a blue ribbon commission created by Congress as a source of fresh ideas—painted a depressingly bleak picture.[45] It was increasingly clear that without significant change, the Democrats would use their control of Congress to force disengagement.

"Although Bush knew the strategy in Iraq was in trouble," Bing West wrote, "he didn't know what to do about it."[46] In a June 2006 Camp David strategy session, Rumsfeld, who still dominated strategy making at that point, continued to advocate a more rapid transition to the ISF.[47] He alone among the administration's key figures had an overarching theory of American global military strategy. The problem was that it was based on quick, decisive applications of high-tech military power, and the Iraq insurgency did not fit within it. Participating by video conference, General Casey advised President Bush that he had adequate forces to train the Iraqis and put them in the lead, but not to hold the cities.[48] He continued to advocate accelerated transition from U.S. to Iraqi military operations. The meeting thus left President Bush where he began— with key advisers advocating continuity in the face of eroding security. No one could explain why continuing to do the same thing would lead to different results.

Following the Camp David meeting, the search for new ideas intensified. On the President's instructions, General Peter Pace, Chairman of the JCS, began a review, relying on a team of veteran colonels. The National Security Council (NSC) instigated its own internal assessment led by Meghan O'Sullivan. Stephen

Hadley had begun to believe that an increase in American troops might be the only way to synchronize the strategy with the President's objectives, but he also knew that Rumsfeld and the uniformed military leaders opposed the idea. Hence he instructed William Luti of the NSC staff—a former Navy officer with a Ph.D. from the Fletcher School of Law and Diplomacy—to assess the feasibility of a troop buildup, but to do so without DoD involvement.[49]

The Democratic victory in the November election added urgency to the search for a new strategy while the resignation of Secretary Rumsfeld immediately afterwards removed one of the obstacles to major change. Altering the Iraq strategy was both imperative and possible. In November and December, the NSC launched a formal interagency strategy review led by Deputy National Security Adviser J. D. Crouch. By December it was clear that the President was leaning toward a troop increase and a shift in mission, but he had not made his final decision. On December 13, 2006, President Bush and Vice President Cheney met the JCS to solicit their input. While the service chiefs were not enthusiastic about a troop increase, Bush assuaged the concerns of General Schoomaker, the Army Chief of Staff, and General James Conway, the Marine Corps Commandant, by supporting an increase in the size of the land forces (which Rumsfeld had opposed).[50]

The questions then were, what should the size of the troop increase be, and what to do with them. Pace and Casey recommended a surge of two Army brigade combat teams and two Marine battalions, with most of the new forces dedicated to training and advising the Iraqis.[51] But President Bush approved the maximum increase that the Pentagon said it could support—five brigades—and, importantly, using them for population security rather than simply training and advising. In a January 10, 2007, press conference, he explained:

> It is clear we need to change our strategy in Iraq. . . . I've committed more than 20,000 additional American troops to Iraq. The vast majority of them — five brigades — will be deployed to Baghdad. These troops will work alongside Iraqi units and be embedded in their formations. Our troops will have a well-defined mission: to help Iraqis clear and secure neighborhoods, to help them protect the local population, and to help ensure the Iraqi forces left behind are capable of providing the security that Baghdad needs.[52]

Thus was born what became popularly known as "the surge."

Decision Shapers.

All strategic decisions have "shapers" both inside the government and outside it. Two types of outsiders were important for the strategic shift of 2007: counterinsurgency experts and policy analysts. The community of experts, although small, played an important role because the U.S. military, the intelligence community, and other government agencies had largely abandoned and forgotten counterinsurgency after the end of the Cold War. The experts, most in the professional military educational system and various Washington research institutes, drew on history to spark the relearning process. For instance, Dr. Kalev Sepp, a former U.S. Army Special Forces officer and veteran of the counterinsurgency campaign in El Salvador who was serving on the faculty of the Naval Postgraduate School, became an adviser to General Casey and penned an article on counterinsurgency "best practices" which helped shape thinking across the Army.[53] Bruce Hoffman and his colleagues at the RAND Corporation reminded political leaders and strategists of counterinsurgency's historical lessons.[54] Experts who had cut their teeth during the Cold War were joined by younger thinkers inside the military. Most important were Lieutenant Colonel John Nagl, whose book on counterinsurgency in Malaya and Vietnam was widely touted within the U.S. military; and Australian Lieutenant Colonel David Kilcullen, who advised General David Petraeus, Casey's replacement as the U.S. commander in Iraq, and who wrote widely on counterinsurgency.[55]

One of the most important contributions from the community of experts was a 2005 article in *Foreign Affairs* by Andrew Krepinevich, president of the Center for Strategic and Budgetary Analysis.[56] Krepinevich, a Ph.D. and former U.S. Army officer, was one of the original conceptualizers of the "revolution in military affairs" during the 1990s and thus understood Secretary Rumsfeld's notion of defense transformation—a phrase Krepinevich helped coin while serving on the National Defense Panel.[57] But having written an influential book on the U.S. Army's performance in Vietnam, he also understood counterinsurgency.[58] His article argued that simply "killing insurgents" did not reflect "the principles of counterinsurgency warfare." Instead, Krepinevich wrote, the U.S. military should "concentrate on providing security and opportunity to the Iraqi people, thereby denying insurgents the popular support they need."[59]

The emphasis on population security reflected the long-standing notion in counterinsurgency strategy—derived primarily from the British and French experience fighting communist and nationalist insurgencies in the 20th century—that separating the insurgents from the population is crucial. Insurgents require at least the acquiescence of the population and prefer active support in terms of information, sanctuary, recruits, and funds. In many insurgencies, the rebels force the population to provide these. This position, in other words, assumes that little of the population willingly supports the insurgents, but is compelled to do so. If security forces protect the population from the insurgents, the support dries up. In fact, the population will actively begin to support the government, most importantly by providing information about the insurgents. From this perspective, population security is not an alternative to offensive operations against the insurgents, but is a vital part of them.

As Krepinevich and other counterinsurgency experts explained, the primary method for protecting the population was what French counterinsurgency experts during the Cold War called the "oil spot" technique in which selected areas were first cleared of insurgents and fully secured, then expanded. This was the inspiration for the "hold" component of the "clear/hold/build" approach which President Bush eventually adopted.

The wider community of policy analysts, commentators, and pundits helped shape the decision environment by providing intellectual ammunition both for the Bush administration and its critics. Those on the political left contended that the Bush strategy was fatally flawed and thus advocated either immediate or rapid withdrawal from Iraq. The most important of these were former Pentagon official Lawrence Korb, a senior fellow at the Center for American Progress; and Steven Simon of the Council on Foreign Relations.[60] A few realist thinkers like Zbigniew

Brzeziński, President Jimmy Carter's National Security Adviser; and retired Lieutenant General William Odom, director of the National Security Agency during the Reagan administration, also advocated disengagement, basing their arguments on the contention that the strategic costs of continued involvement outweighed the expected strategic benefits.[61]

Because of its senior participants and bipartisan composition, the Iraq Study Group attracted the most attention among the outside groups.[62] Opponents of U.S. involvement in Iraq hoped the Study Group would win over some of the Bush administration's less committed supporters to their position. The administration itself initially believed the Study Group would bolster its position but eventually recognized that this would not happen. The group's final report—released in December 2006—advocated withdrawal with the minimum strategic damage rather than decisive victory. While President Bush indicated that he would seriously consider the study group's advice, he did not adopt its major recommendations such as a diplomatic initiative to engage Iran and Syria, and linking the Israeli-Palestinian conflict to the one in Iraq.[63] Still, the study group's criticism of existing strategy must have influenced Bush's thinking. It was one thing when the political left criticized the war; that criticism the administration could disregard. It was something altogether different when esteemed experts and experienced leaders from across the political spectrum did so. This probably made President Bush more amenable to high risk options since increasing the U.S. troop presence soon would be politically infeasible. In strategy, negative trends often increase the risk tolerance of decisionmakers.

Meanwhile, the political right worked to maintain public and congressional support for the Bush strategy. While the noisiest components—like talk radio and cable news pundits—focused on the mass public, the most important was a group of experts associated with the American Enterprise Institute (AEI), particularly military scholar Frederick Kagan and retired U.S. Army Vice Chief of Staff General John Keane. Keane's involvement was important. In a September 2006 meeting with Secretary Rumsfeld and a December meeting with President Bush, Keane argued that there was a serious gap between the President's declared goal of decisive victory and the way the U.S. military was being employed in Iraq.[64] He was realistic that there would be a short-term spike in casualties with the increased numbers of troops and the new approach, but believed that was a necessary price of long-term success.[65] That this came from a very experienced military officer showed that there were multiple positions even among military experts—something that Rumsfeld had kept hidden by ensuring that he and the uniformed senior leaders spoke with one voice. Since Keane was retired, he could be brutally frank. In all likelihood, President Bush had not heard senior military leaders warning of outright defeat or advocating a politically unpopular troop increase while Rumsfeld controlled the flow of information.

In the autumn of 2006, Keane and Kagan led an AEI study group which eventually advocated a major troop increase and a shift in mission to population security and controlling the sectarian violence in Baghdad.[66] Unless this was done, the group's report contended, it was impossible to train and advise the ISF or crush al Qaeda. This approach had profound implications. It would not only add a new task—quelling Iraq's civil war—but would also reshuffle the priorities among existing missions. The key was population security. While experts long argued that this was the centerpiece of counterinsurgency, and U.S. military doctrine codified the idea, American strategy in Iraq did not reflect it. Instead, it delegated population security to the ISF, which were unable or unwilling to do it.[67] Thus, the AEI group concluded, U.S. strategy was at variance with U.S. doctrine. It went on to suggest both how additional troops should be employed and how the military might make them available. While the AEI report did not lead President Bush in new directions, it made him aware of the feasibility of a surge, despite less enthusiasm from the Pentagon or CENTCOM (both of which were convinced that a troop increase would have a tactical effect but not a strategic one without a parallel effort to translate improved security into political gains). As with the initial development of American nuclear strategy in the 1940s and 1950s and the creation of counterinsurgency strategy in the 1960s, the community of nongovernment experts was an important source of ideas unconstrained by bureaucratic or organizational imperatives. Traditionally, much of the creativity in American strategy comes from outside the formal system.

As debate raged and the various assessments moved forward, dissatisfaction grew in Congress. Most Democrats favored an immediate or quick withdrawal from Iraq, contending that the cause was lost. A few legislators—most importantly Senator John McCain (R-AZ)— favored an increased U.S. military presence. Like Hadley and Keane, McCain believed that the existing strategy did not reflect President Bush's objectives. But he was in the minority, increasingly even within his own party. By 2006, a number of

25

moderate Republicans like Lindsay Graham (R-SC), George Allen (R-VA), Kay Bailey Hutchinson (R-TX), Chuck Hagel (R-NE), Lincoln Chafee (R-RI), and Olympia Snowe (R-ME) expressed dissatisfaction with the conduct of the war.[68] Like the Iraq Study Group, this showed President Bush that time was running out on his existing strategy, leaving him with little hope that he could sustain support for it in the absence of clear progress.

The discipline of the Bush White House makes it difficult to assess who among the President's senior advisers had the greatest influence on Iraq strategy. Hadley was extremely important, working closely with General Pace to navigate the tricky civil-military aspects of the shift. Vice President Cheney likely played a major role. Following the September 11, 2001 (9/11) attacks, he had been the leader of the administration's hard liners, pushing for armed intervention to remove Saddam Hussein and most actively portraying Iraq as the front line in the conflict with al Qaeda.[69] It is difficult, though, to know exactly how Cheney shaped the President's thinking on the strategic shift of 2007.[70] Their consultations were private, and Cheney was the ultimate loyalist who would never indicate any divergence with the President even if it existed. Publicly, his role was to rally support for the administration.

Both as National Security Adviser and, later, as Secretary of State, Condoleezza Rice was clearly a close confidant of the President and undoubtedly shaped his thinking on Iraq. In the initial period of the Iraq insurgency, though, Rice did not appear to be a major player (although, of course, it is impossible to know at this point what her role was behind the scenes). As Bob Woodward put it, "Rice and Hadley, her deputy at the time, had worked on Iraq nonstop, and yet they never got control over the policy making. They were no match for Rumsfeld."[71] The only public instance where Rice staked out a position that clearly propelled the administration's thinking was in a November 2005 Senate testimony when she described existing policy as a "clear/hold/build" approach.[72] Woodward contends that Secretary Rice had not discussed this with Generals Abizaid or Casey, or with Secretary Rumsfeld, and that it ran counter to their support for a diminution of U.S. involvement in holding secured areas and handing them over Iraqi forces.[73] But President Bush quickly picked up on the phrase, thus making it part of U.S. strategy.

There is little indication that the Chairmen of the JCS—Air Force General Richard Myers, and later, Marine General Peter Pace—had significant influence on broad strategic decisions. Despite the fact that, by law, the Chairman serves as the primary military adviser to the President, Secretary Rumsfeld insisted on serving as the conduit for military advice and assured that he and the Chairman spoke with one voice. The other Service chiefs—who again have statutory roles as advisers to the President—had very little direct access to President Bush and appeared to play a minimal role in shaping U.S. strategy in Iraq.[74]

Decision Criteria and Dynamics.

The dominant decision criteria in the strategic shift of 2007 were identifying clear, unambiguous victory as the overarching objective (thus ruling out a negotiated settlement, which often happens in counterinsurgency), and the priority accorded to Iraq within the broader scope of American strategy. The definition of victory had not changed since its articulation in the

Bush administration's 2005 *National Strategy for Victory in Iraq*:

- Victory in Iraq is Defined in Stages
  - *Short term*: Iraq is making steady progress in fighting terrorists, meeting political milestones, building democratic institutions, and standing up security forces.
  - *Medium term*: Iraq is in the lead defeating terrorists and providing its own security, with a fully constitutional government in place, and on its way to achieving its economic potential.
  - *Longer term*: Iraq is peaceful, united, stable, and secure, well integrated into the international community, and a full partner in the global war on terrorism.
- Victory in Iraq is a Vital U.S. Interest
  - Iraq is the central front in the global war on terror. Failure in Iraq will embolden terrorists and expand their reach; success in Iraq will deal them a decisive and crippling blow.
  - The fate of the greater Middle East—which will have a profound and lasting impact on American security—hangs in the balance.
- Failure is Not an Option
  - Iraq would become a safe haven from which terrorists could plan attacks against America, American interests abroad, and our allies.
  - Middle East reformers would never again fully trust American assurances of support for democracy and human rights in the region—a historic opportunity lost.
  - The resultant tribal and sectarian chaos would have major consequences for American security and interests in the region.[75]

But while the end state remained constant, the time horizon changed. President Bush recognized that the existing approach was not leading toward victory rapidly enough given eroding support for American involvement in Iraq. This left two options: accept the pressure for withdrawal with the foreknowledge that this was unlikely to lead to victory as defined in the 2005 strategy; or pursue a "game changer" that might shift the dynamics of the conflict. But, Bush knew, the window of opportunity for a game changer was closing. This increased his willingness to accept increased short-term risk in order to preserve the chance of long-term success.

President Bush's overall decisionmaking style was similar to that of Ronald Reagan: he set broad strategic objectives, gave general guidance, and then let advisers develop the details. He was less involved in the specifics than some of his predecessors, like Clinton. Such a method is effective *if* the president is given a full range of options and an assessment of the strengths, weaknesses, costs, and risks of each. Reagan had a diverse group of assertive senior advisers who provided this. No single adviser dominated. Until 2006, this was less evident in the Bush administration. Secretary Rumsfeld, with the support of Vice President Cheney, dominated strategy making. The uniformed military, including the two JCS chairmen, did not provide an independent perspective. Other figures who might have played a major role—Secretary of State Powell until his resignation in 2005 and Condoleezza Rice in her role as National Security Adviser and then Secretary of State—could not counter Rumsfeld and Cheney (who were backed by the uniformed military).

As the security situation in Iraq eroded, Rumsfeld's influence declined. From 2003 to 2006, Iraq was "Mr.

Rumsfeld's war." With Rumsfeld fading, President Bush became more directive. Initially, he was hesitant to overrule advice from uniformed military leaders. But Bush opted for the maximum troop increase and shift in mission priority to population security even though the Service chiefs, Pace, Abizaid, and Casey were, at best, unenthusiastic. As Bing West put it:

> It was Hadley and the NSC staff . . . who had orchestrated the surge by quietly gathering a consensus among insiders, especially [then-Lieutenant General Raymond] Odierno, Pace, and Petraeus, and outsiders. . . . while Keane added the stature of a four-star general and Kagan contributed concrete specifics.[76]

Options Considered.

As the Bush administration developed and assessed strategic options in the second half of 2006, it grappled with three important unknowns. The first was whether Maliki could or would control his fellow Shiites, particularly the *Jaish al Mahdi* forces of Muqtada al-Sadr, and other sectarian militias involved in violence against Sunni Arabs. As West put it, the core problem was "the feckless performance by Maliki and his government."[77] This involved two interrelated questions—whether Maliki was *capable* of exerting control over the Shiite militias given his limited experience at high level political leadership, and whether he was *interested* in doing so. This was simply the latest manifestation of an enduring problem the United States faces in counterinsurgency support: finding a partner who is effective and committed to resolving the root causes of the conflict. When Washington was able to do this—Napoleon Duarte in

El Salvador or Ramón Magsaysay in the Philippines —
it met with some success. When America's partner
was ineffective or more committed to retaining power
and rewarding clients than addressing the deep
problems that fueled the insurgency (such as Ngo
Dinh Diem, Nguyen Van Thieu, or any of South
Vietnam's other despots), the counterinsurgency effort
failed. In 2006, it was not clear whether Maliki was a
Duarte/Magsaysay or a Diem/Thieu. Despite concern
from senior officials like Rice and Hadley, President
Bush remained convinced that Maliki was capable of
and dedicated to controlling the Shiite militias, and
based his decisions on this assumption.[78]

A second important unknown was whether the
Sunni Arabs recognized that they could not regain
domination of Iraq by violence and would accept
American protection. If they did, assigning U.S. forces
to population security was viable. If not, it would
fail. Since there was no way to accurately gauge
this, President Bush and his advisers had to rely on
assumptions. As it turned out, the assumption that
the Sunni Arab community was willing to accept an
increased American military presence was correct. In
strategy, doing the right thing at the wrong time is as
much a recipe for failure as doing the wrong thing.
Committing U.S. military forces to population security
prior to 2006 would not have worked because neither
the Sunni Arabs nor the Shiites wanted it. Both seemed
to believe that they could attain national dominance.
By 2006, though, the two communities, particularly
the Sunni Arabs, seemed to have reached a level of
fear, desperation and exhaustion that made them
amenable to having the American military in their
neighborhoods. That had become a lesser evil than the
presence of al Qaeda extremists and Shiite militias.

The third important unknown was whether there was enough remaining support among the American public and Congress to sustain an increase in troop levels and spike in casualties, particularly since this would take some time before producing results. Poll numbers suggested otherwise but President Bush believed that he could mobilize and sustain backing for a troop surge. Moreover, Bush had often made clear that he would disregard polls when he was convinced of the rightness of an unpopular action.

Over the summer, the NSC informal policy review developed a range of options:

- Adjust on the margins (i.e., continue with the current approach on the assumption that the ISF would reach a point where they could conduct the counterinsurgency campaign with limited U.S. help before support from the American people and Congress collapsed);
- Target efforts (i.e., continue to attack al Qaeda in Iraq but stay out of the sectarian conflict);
- Double down (i.e., increase troop levels and assistance and attempt to broker the raging sectarian conflict); or
- Bet on Maliki (i.e., write off the Sunni Arab community and simply strengthen the Maliki government to the point that it could crush resistance).[79]

The "double down" option had led National Security Adviser Hadley to ask William Luti if this was feasible given the strains on the military. The NSC did not want to debate options that could not be implemented.

Later, General Pace's JCS study also focused on four options:

1. "Go Big" (i.e., an increase in U.S. forces);

2. "Go Home" (disengagement and withdrawal);

3. "Go Long" (a smaller U.S. military footprint and increased emphasis on the advisory and training mission); and,

4. A hybrid which combined components of the other options.

However, the Service chiefs remained skeptical of a troop increase since it was not clear to them how this would be linked to the attainment of political objectives. As a result, General Pace's study went forward with only one of the options which had been developed by the "Council of Colonels" who built the assessment: continuing the existing approach—with its emphasis on training and advice—but on an accelerated schedule.

According to a former NSC staff member, even though General Pace was sympathetic toward the idea of a troop increase and more direct U.S. involvement in population security, he did not feel that he could overrule his field commanders and the Service chiefs by recommending an option they did not support.[80] This reflects an enduring conundrum for the Chairman of the JCS: he has both an *individual* role as an adviser to the President and an *institutional* role as the senior member of the uniformed military. Senior civilian officials with dual roles, such as the Secretary of State or Secretary of Defense, always emphasize their individual role as presidential advisers rather than their institutional role as the leader of an organization. There is no question that loyalty to the President takes priority over their responsibility to their institution.

For the Chairman, things are not so clear. Only Colin Powell, while serving as Chairman of the Joint Chiefs, overtly leaned toward his individual rather than his institutional role. This duality inherently limits the influence of the Chairman with the President.

At an even broader level, the limited impact of the Chairman's Iraq study demonstrated one of the deepest shortcomings of the American system for strategy development: the lack of an adequate method to integrate political and military planning. The NSC deconflicts, but does not integrate. The military's vast planning apparatus was not optimized for political planning. To the extent it was able to do this, it did so because of the political understanding of individual planners—something that may or may not be available when needed. On the other hand, the State Department and NSC were better equipped for political planning, but their military expertise was coincidental rather than institutional or ingrained. Eventually this shortcoming was overcome because some influential military leaders like General David Petraeus developed an astute sense of the political component of strategy making, and some individuals on the policy side like William Luti understood military planning. But again, this was due more to serendipity and luck than to systemic design. In this case, the system worked but there is no assurance it will in the future short of a major redesign which effectively integrates political and military planning.

During the formal NSC strategy assessment in November and December, the DoD representatives (Stephen Cambone and Peter Rodman), although more open to a troop increase with Secretary Rumsfeld gone, continued to push an accelerated transition to the ISF. This was inspired by the strain that the Iraq conflict continued to place on the military's ability to sustain other U.S. security commitments.[81] The Department of State worried that Maliki would not or could not control the Shiite militias.[82] One of the enduring dilemmas of counterinsurgency support is that the greater the American commitment to a particular leader or regime, the less leverage Washington has. The State Department was searching for the "sweet spot" which would compel Maliki to rein in the Shiite extremists without making him believe that the United States was about to abandon him (which might have encouraged him to cut a deal with extremists, or conversely to attempt a crackdown on the Sunni Arab community). Secretary Rice was also concerned that focusing so much of America's attention and resources on Iraq had adverse effects elsewhere in the world. She favored a broad shift in American strategy to make it less Iraq-centric. The State Department representative in the strategic assessment promoted this idea. Finally John Hannah, Vice President Cheney's representative at the NSC review, was skeptical of Shiite-Sunni reconciliation and advocated clearly backing the Shiites.[83] He did, however, support the idea of a troop increase.

Ultimately President Bush rejected major shifts in the *political* component of his administration's approach to Iraq and continued full support for the Maliki government, while encouraging it to reconcile with the Sunni Arab community and expand economic development. The heart of the strategic shift was a *military* decision based on two separate but linked components: troop levels and mission priorities. One position held that more U.S. forces were needed whether the mission was population security or training and advice. Another was that many Iraqis saw U.S. military forces as alien occupiers, and thus the fewer of them the better. In addition, U.S. forces were a crutch for the Iraqi government and security forces, allowing them to postpone or avoid difficult decisions and actions.[84] Diminishing the size of the American presence, according to this argument, would compel the Iraqis to do what they needed to do.

These two components combined to form four discrete strategic options (see Figure 1):

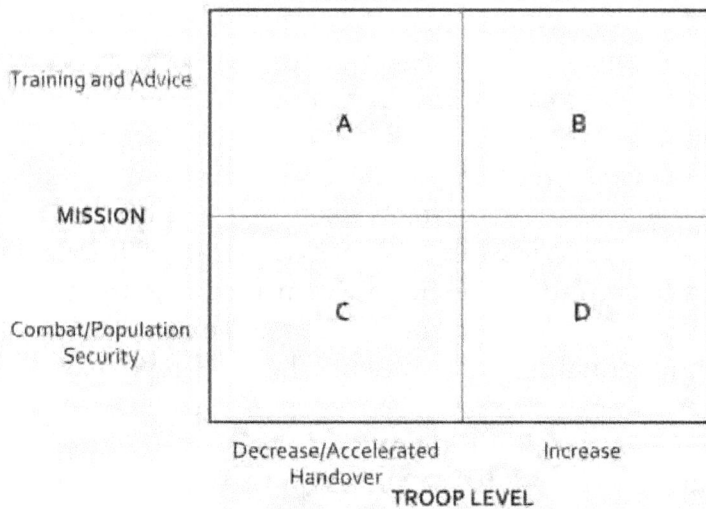

Figure 1. The Four Strategic Options.

To some extent, the two elements of the decision were sequential: The administration first had to decide what it intended to do with American forces before it could assess the number needed to perform the mission.

Excluding those who favored immediate disengagement (primarily on the political left), blocks A and D had the most support. For instance, Abizaid and Casey favored block A: training and advice with a troop level that diminished as Iraqi capabilities increased.[85] The Iraq Study Group also fell within block A, advocating an increase in the number of U.S. military advisers and trainers but an overall decrease in American troop numbers.[86] A few commentators and military leaders favored block B. Nevertheless, President Bush opted for block D, concluding that it was feasible and optimized the chances for victory as he defined it.

ANALYSIS

Following President Bush's announcement of the strategic shift, General Casey and Ambassador Khalilzad began preparation for the shift to include steps to ensure that Iraqi security forces would successfully fulfill their role in sustaining security in areas cleared by the American military. Full implementation of the revised strategy began just as General Petraeus replaced General Casey as the overall American military commander in Iraq. This transition in leadership of the Iraq effort had been planned for months (although its exact timing was left open) and was not itself part of the strategic shift, but did facilitate it. It was a new face for what was being portrayed and seen as a "new" strategy.[87] Petraeus created a Joint Strategic Assessment Team and in July 2007 formally adopted a Joint Campaign Plan which assigned most of the newly arrived troops to population security.[88] General Petraeus and U.S. Ambassador Ryan Crocker developed cease fires with key Iraqi individuals and organizations.[89] The military component of the plan—made possible by the arrival of the five surge brigades—was combined with governance, development, and improved infra-structure protection. Under then-Lieutenant General

Raymond Odierno, commander of the Multi-National Corps-Iraq (MNC-I), U.S. forces secured the approaches to and "belts" around Baghdad, and established a permanent presence in neighborhoods in conflict.

Capitalizing on growing rifts within the insurgency, particularly between al Qaeda and Sunni Arab tribal leaders, mid-level American commanders had since 2005 developed relationships with the Sunni Arab militias and eventually put 20,000 of their fighters on the U.S. payroll, using them to deter, control, or eradicate al Qaeda extremists.[90] High value targeting programs implemented by U.S. special operations forces, regular military units, and the intelligence community became more effective, in part because of the increased intelligence gained by involvement with population security.[91] By the end of the summer of 2007, overall violence, particularly sectarian attacks, was in decline. Security in Baghdad and other violent areas improved dramatically, and President Maliki did rise to the occasion and rein in support for sectarian violence from within his government and security forces. In contrast to the Baghdad security operations of 2006, the ISF proved more effective, and there was a political program to consolidate the gains.

The popular perception is that the troop surge snatched victory from the jaws of defeat.[92] In reality the timing of the strategic shift was as crucial as its content. By the end of 2006, a "perfect storm" of trends and conditions had altered the trajectory of the conflict. It is certainly true that nearly all Iraqis were, by that point, tired of violence. This was vital. The American approach to counterinsurgency — as codified in military doctrine and interagency guidance — assumes that the population is hostile to the insurgents but tolerates them out of fear.[93] Hence the solution is protecting the population from the insurgents, preferably using local security forces. In reality, populations sometimes prefer the insurgents over the government even though the government can provide more resources, at least in the short term. In Iraq, many or most Sunni Arabs initially supported the insurgents or at least were passively sympathetic to them. But they grew disillusioned. As West put it, "By November of 2006, the will of the people—that essential ingredient in defeating an insurgency—had turned the war in favor of the coalition. . . . The change in attitude of the Sunni [Arab] population and the momentum in a dozen cities had come from the bottom up, from the tribes and battalions."[94] Only with the shift in attitude did using U.S. troops for population security become feasible. The schism between Iraqi tribes and the extremists further fueled the loss of faith in the insurgency.

The decision by Muqtada al-Sadr to order the forces loyal to him to avoid confrontation with American troops as the surge began, and later, his August 2007 declaration of a truce were vital. While al Qaeda in Iraq—like Cold War communist insurgents—sought decisive victory and control of the state, Sadr's Shiite militias (and some of the local Sunni Arab insurgent groups) were more akin to Hezbollah, using violence to force their way into the political system rather than attempting to replace it. By 2007, Sadr seemed to have recognized that with the increased size and effectiveness of the American military in Iraq, improvements in the Iraqi security forces, and the growing competence of the Maliki government, he had gotten as far as he could with violence. Maliki's assertiveness, in turn, may have come from his reading of the American political situation. With the Democratic electoral victory in November 2006, and the leaking of Hadley's memo, Maliki must have known that he had to control extremists in his government or risk losing American support.[95] Luckily for him, global increases in oil prices left his government flush with money, allowing it to buy support or acquiescence from key organizations, groups, and constituencies.

One of the most important enablers of the strategic shift of 2007 was the tremendous improvement that the American military and intelligence community had undergone during the 4 years of the conflict. From enlisted Soldiers and Marines to general officers, there was deeper experience; better equipment and training; better cultural and situational awareness; better doctrine; and better tactics, techniques, and procedures. This meant that the force of 2007 was able to do things—like population security through permanent presence and effective high value targeting—that the force of 2003-05 could not. The strategic shift not only involved *more* troops, but also *better* ones. In all likelihood, the 2005 American force could not have implemented the 2007 strategy even if it had tried.

From 2004 to 2006, the Iraq conflict changed from a predominantly anti-American insurgency to one dominated by a sectarian war stoked by outside extremists. When the conflict was purely an anti-American insurgency, a strategy focused on strengthening Iraqi security forces and minimizing the American role was correct. But by 2006, the insurgents had seized the strategic initiative and changed the nature of the conflict. Thus the strategy of 2004-05 was no longer appropriate. Counterinsurgency support works best with the smallest possible footprint for foreign forces, and that was exactly what the United States attempted up to 2006. But *peacekeeping*—which is the appropriate response to a sectarian or ethnic civil war—demands a significant presence of outside forces to play the role of mediator. That was a crucial part of the strategic shift of 2007: the U.S. military changed from pure counterinsurgency support to counterinsurgency support *plus* peacekeeping.

Recognition of this was slow because the insurgency persisted even while the sectarian war exploded. The counterinsurgency mission was not replaced by a peacekeeping mission, but a peacekeeping mission joined the counterinsurgency mission. In reality, both the insurgency and sectarian conflict had been present in Iraq from the time Saddam Hussein was removed from power. What had changed by 2006 was the relative priority of the two as sectarian conflict became the more important. This created political problems for the Bush administration. Sustaining public and congressional support for counterinsurgency is inherently difficult, but at least the involvement of al Qaeda and the barbarism of insurgents like Zarqawi gave the administration some political ammunition. Selling the American public and Congress on peacekeeping or peace enforcement is even harder—witness the fragility of support for intervention in Somalia, Rwanda, Congo, or the Balkans during the 1990s. President Bush himself had expressed his opposition to using the U.S. military for peacekeeping during the 2000 campaign. This meant the administration had to portray the strategic shift as a more effective method of *counterinsurgency*. It could not use the word "peacekeeping," even though that was exactly what it was doing. Ultimately, it was a close call. Had the strategic shift not come at precisely the right time to generate quick results—if not for the "perfect storm" of conditions—the administration would not have been able to sustain adequate public and congressional support. Congress probably would have mandated disengagement in late 2007, or early 2008, even without a demonstrable decline in violence.

In any case, the evidence does not support the contention that the United States pursued an ineffective strategy until 2007, then suddenly discovered an effective one. The approach implemented in 2007 would not have worked even a year earlier because all of the necessary conditions were not in place. And it probably would not have had the same results had it been undertaken a year later.[96] In strategy, nations must not only do the right thing, but must do the right thing at the right time. This is certainly true of the strategic shift of 2007. It capitalized on a temporary and volatile combination of trends and conditions. It was the right approach at the right time. While experts argue over whether it is better to be good or lucky in strategy, the United States was both reasonably good *and* lucky in Iraq.

IMPLICATIONS

The strategic shift of 2007 offers important insight into the dynamics of American strategy formulation, particularly the dynamics of civil-military relations and the role of the uniformed military in strategy making. To be truly effective, strategy requires intimate presidential involvement. Yet nothing assures that the President will have expertise in national security or even a talent for it. If anything, an interest in foreign affairs is an electoral liability (at least since the end of the Cold War). Some Presidents grow into the role of strategist-in-chief, but nothing in the American political system assures this. Historically, a few Presidents developed strategic talent and personally dominated strategy making. Lincoln during the Civil War and Franklin Roosevelt during World War II are examples. Others never developed great strategic skill but nonetheless insisted on dominating strategy formulation. Johnson, Carter, and Clinton fall into this category. A few Presidents subcontract strategy to a single adviser (Nixon and Ford with Kissinger). Others rely on multiple advisers in a collective strategy-making process. This would include Reagan, George H. W. Bush, and, until the summer of 2006 when Rumsfeld's and Cheney's influence declined, George W. Bush. Like Lincoln or Roosevelt, George W. Bush assumed greater personal control of strategy making as the conflict he directed continued. In general, Presidents become more intimately involved in strategy making over the course of their administration. Obviously, two-term Presidents will have more time to assume this role than those who serve a single term.

With rare exceptions, significant strategic shifts are only possible when a President has deferred to an adviser or coterie of advisers. This is because it is very difficult for a President to admit that his earlier positions were flawed. Doing so can be politically disastrous, as when Carter admitted he had been wrong about the Soviets following the 1979 invasion of Afghanistan. An open *mea culpa* would erode the effectiveness of even a President not facing reelection. But if a failed or ineffective strategy can be attributed to an adviser or group of advisers who are then replaced, the President can forge a new path with less political damage. That is exactly what happened in 2006 when Cheney moved to the background and Rumsfeld resigned, allowing President Bush to adjust his strategy without having to admit that his previous one was misguided. Bush's admirers talk disparagingly of the "Rumsfeld strategy" or the "Rumsfeld-Abizaid-Casey strategy" before 2007 rather than the *Bush* strategy. Bush's problem, for the Bush admirers, was only that he trusted Rumsfeld and the military commanders too much, not that he failed to understand Iraq and its conflict. This is an alibi, not an explanation.

The strategic shift of 2007 suggested that military leaders often have a more expansive strategic and time perspective than Presidents. This can be a source of dissonance or tension. American Presidents think in 4-year periods with an eye on their own legacy. Senior military leaders, most of whom have spent 30 years or more in an institution which cultivates and sustains intense loyalty, are more prone to consider how their actions will affect the nation, the military, and the long-term future of their Service. One simple indicator of this divergent perspective is the fact that the DoD and the Services have programs to assess the strategic environment and armed conflict years or decades into the future. No President devotes much time to American strategy 10 or 20 years hence. To put it in military jargon, Presidents are focused on the strategic "close battle" while the military simultaneously considers both the "close" and "deep" battles. Because military leaders see themselves as the embodiment of their Service and the military in general, rather than simply individuals, and because the Services existed before them and will exist after them, they are less consumed with leaving their personal mark on history than on being the steward of their Service. The result is a persistent asymmetry in risk tolerance. This was clear in American strategy toward Iraq: Bush and Rumsfeld were more risk tolerant than most of the senior military leaders.

The debates leading to the strategic shift of 2007

demonstrated this. The outcome in Iraq was clearly and dominantly President Bush's top priority. History will judge him by it. The military, particularly the Service chiefs, were certainly committed to the President's objectives in Iraq but were also concerned with the long-term health of their organizations and the broader span of America's global commitments. They sought success in Iraq but not at the expense of wrecking their Services. They were, in a sense, more tolerant of risk in Iraq, if accepting it lowered the long-term risk to the health of their Services. Presidents and defense secretaries recognize the competing pressures on Service chiefs and take this into account when receiving their advice. This is a major reason that the collective JCS had a minimal role in the initial decision to intervene in Iraq and in the strategic shift of 2007. Certainly President Bush considered them important stakeholders and, during the strategic review, expended great effort to gain their backing for the shift. But as is always the case when the uniformed military's perspective differs from the President's, the President wins. The JCS knew this and acceded to the strategic shift in Iraq once it became clear that President Bush was committed to it.

In any case, military advice is only effective when the President and Secretary of Defense want it to be. If civilian leaders are confident that they can craft strategy with limited military input, they can easily do so. While President Bush was receptive to military advice on operational issues but not broad strategy, Secretary Rumsfeld was convinced that the uniformed military was too hidebound and uncreative to adopt the sort of bold approach he advocated.[97] Even though the Goldwater-Nichols Reform Act of 1986 gave the JCS, particularly the Chairman, a direct channel to the President, it did not guarantee that the

Service chiefs would use it, or more importantly, that policymakers would take any advice they received. Secretary Rumsfeld—like most of America's defense secretaries—would not have tolerated military leaders developing a direct and independent relationship with President Bush. He insisted, for instance, on seeing any briefing that General Casey intended to give President Bush beforehand.[98] Based on available information, this limitation also applied to the Chairman—there is no indication of either General Myers or General Pace giving President Bush advice or counsel at variance with Secretary Rumsfeld's.[99] Some past presidents like Franklin Roosevelt and Bill Clinton were known for developing direct contacts with military and civilian officials below the cabinet level. President Bush only did this in a limited way, primarily with Franks, Casey, Petraeus, and Bremer.[100] Even then Rumsfeld, Cheney, and Rice or Hadley were normally present during the discussion.

This is a recurring issue in American strategy making. In describing policymaking during the war in Vietnam, H. R. McMaster wrote:

> While they slowly deepened American military involvement in Vietnam, Johnson and McNamara pushed the Chiefs further away from the decisionmaking process. There was no meaningful structure through which the Chiefs could voice their views—even the Chairman was not a reliable conduit....Rather than advice, McNamara and Johnson extracted from the JCS acquiescence and silent support for decisions already made. Even as they relegated the Chiefs to a peripheral position in the policy-making process, they were careful to preserve the facade of consultation to prevent the JCS from opposing the administration's policies either openly or behind the scenes.[101]

If "Iraq" is substituted for "Vietnam," and "Bush and Rumsfeld" for "Johnson and McNamara," this still rings true. The common variable was the personality of the Secretary of Defense: both Rumsfeld and McNamara were brilliant, aggressive, confident leaders who saw little need for strategic advice from the uniformed military. Senior military leaders were implementers, not strategy makers. There may be a future defense secretary who follows this pattern, again limiting the uniformed military to the realm of operations rather than national strategy. The regional and field commanders in Iraq did have regular access to the President, but even had they been inclined to diverge from Secretary Rumsfeld on broader questions of national strategy, they were proscribed by a sense of their own role and duty from doing so. It was at this broader level where the most important problems resided, not with the military operations.

The limited role of the uniformed military in framing broad national strategy was not peculiar to Iraq and will persist in the future. Neither the Joint Chiefs nor regional combatant commanders are appointed on the basis of strategic prowess. Some, perhaps most of them, are in fact astute strategists, but the system does not select for that quality and hence does not assure it.[102] Of course the President and Secretary of Defense are not necessarily selected for strategic prowess either, but they get to shape it nonetheless. The American political system assumes that astute strategists will emerge when needed. Often they do, but that is a shaky foundation for a great power. Further discussion and debate are needed to consider how to select both senior military leaders and civilian policymakers for strategic expertise. Given the complex nature of strategic expertise and talent, this would be extraordinarily difficult, but that is not a reason to avoid trying.

If the members of the JCS or combatant commanders do not have a firm grasp of strategy, it becomes even easier for a President or Secretary of Defense disinclined to take military advice seriously to disregard it. Even so, military advice on national strategy would be more effective if it harnessed both the Service chiefs and the combatant commanders. President Bush and Secretary Rumsfeld considered the combatant commanders more independent of institutional Service interests than the Joint Chiefs, and thus were more amenable to their strategic advice. This is likely to persist in future presidential administrations. Hence Congress should consider creating a permanent strategic council—led by the Chairman—which integrates the views of both the combatant commanders and the Service chiefs. If designed to deal with only broad strategy, this would not have to meet more than a few times a year (the Secretary of Defense normally convenes such a council of combatant commanders and Service chiefs several times a year, but this is an informal process). Any legislation which created such a council should also specify methods to assure that its advice at least reaches the President. The United States is not best served when a senior military leader's career requires parroting the Secretary of Defense.

The military's involvement in strategy making is not limited to advice from senior leaders to policymakers. The military has a multitude of talented strategists and subject matter experts who work throughout the DoD and, to a lesser extent, other government agencies. Their role, though, varies according to the preferences of the presidential administration. Some administrations and some civilian policymakers place great stock in professional expertise and rely on it during decisionmaking. Others value commitment to the administration's objectives, priorities, assumptions, and perceptions more than professional expertise. This is a result of the overlap between strategy and policy, or more accurately, strategy and politics. There is general agreement that the uniformed military should play a role in *strategy* formulation, but that it should be less involved or uninvolved in making *policy*. The problem is that each presidential administration distinguishes strategy and policy differently. The military's influence is not determined solely by the talent and expertise that it brings to the table, but by the way an administration defines strategy and policy.

As with all large organizations, creativity and a spirit of innovation in the military is maximized at what might be called the "upper middle" level, and diminishes at the most senior levels. In particular, the greatest creativity in the military tends to be at the senior field grade ranks: lieutenant colonels/ commanders and colonels/captains. Below that, officers do not have the experience and expertise to adequately refine creative ideas or the rank to make their voices heard. Above that, competing pressures combine to compel leaders toward more risk averse decisions. That the Service chiefs jettisoned all of the options developed by the JCS "Council of Colonels" — except the one calling for continuity — supports this argument. The clear implication is that innovative thinkers at the upper middle level must have venues for communicating their ideas in a way that will not damage their career prospects.[103]

The strategic shift of 2007 in Iraq demonstrated that even if the military is the secondary or supporting element of American strategy – and the core problems in Iraq were political – the military dimension will attract the most scrutiny and be the most controversial. The intentions and competence of the Maliki government were much more important than American force levels in determining the outcome in Iraq. But military force levels received significantly more media coverage and discussion within the United States. This is unfortunate but unavoidable. American military leaders must be aware that, like Hollywood celebrities, their every action and statement will be parsed, debated, and critiqued. Involvement in counterinsurgency – a type of protracted conflict imbued with ambiguity which does not reflect the American strategic culture – exacerbates the problem. For example, Americans are impatient by nature. Without regular progress in an overseas endeavor, support wavers, and can crumble. But in counterinsurgency, months or years often pass with little discernible progress. Because insurgency and counterinsurgency are primarily psychological, it is often hard to measure progress (or regression). This places U.S. military leaders, who will normally be the face of the American effort, in an extraordinarily difficult position as they attempt to provide a realistic portrayal of events while sustaining public and congressional support. At times it may be impossible. Presidents may then find that replacing the military commander is the least painful way of demonstrating initiative in the face of crumbling public and congressional support. Phrased differently, senior U.S. military commanders in counterinsurgency campaigns may be removed for political and psychological reasons even when their performance is as good as possible under the circumstances. As President Bush told journalist Bob Woodward when discussing the strategic shift of 2007, "new people to implement the new strategy is an exclamation point on new strategy."[104] Replacing military commanders when the public and Congress grow restive with what they consider inadequate progress is an American tradition— witness McClellan, Hooker, Burnside, MacArthur, and McKiernan. The political and psychological intensity of counterinsurgency means that commanders will be given even less leeway than those involved in conventional warfighting. There is nothing the military can do about this: it is an occupational hazard.

Most often, though, this will only apply to the most senior commander in the field. One of the conundrums the United States faces when engaged in large scale counterinsurgency is that the American military prefers to rotate commanders fairly quickly, but counterinsurgency is most successful when commanders (and troops) have extensive experience in their operating area. Long tours—perhaps even for the duration of the conflict—would maximize effectiveness, but could damage the quality of the military and limit the promotion potential of officers who need command time. In Iraq, the DoD settled on a compromise: brigade and battalion commanders rotated after a year but the senior commanders, such as General Casey, stayed for longer periods of time.[105] This meant that senior commanders became the face of the American effort, and thus were susceptible to blame as frustration mounted within the American public and Congress. Again, this is likely to persist so long as the United States undertakes protracted irregular campaigns, whether counterinsurgency or something else.

A commander faces immense challenges in counterinsurgency, in part because it is a quintessentially psychological form of conflict. His skill as a communicator is as or more important than his skill as a commander. Take, for instance, the complex messages that the U.S. commander in Iraq needed to transmit:

- To the U.S. public and Congress:
  - The stakes in Iraq are extensive: the effort is worthwhile;
  - The United States and the Iraqi government are making significant progress in the security, economic, and political realms;
  - There is an identifiable end state after which American involvement will be minimal;
  - Every effort is being made to limit U.S. casualties.
- To the Iraqi government and security forces:
  - The U.S. commitment is steadfast but conditional on continued progress and reform;
  - The United States has no desire to dominate or exploit Iraq, or preserve a long-term military presence.
- To the Iraqi people:
  - The Iraqi government and security forces seek their best interests;
  - The Iraqi government and security forces are improving and soon will no longer need extensive American support;
  - The insurgents are the source of violence and instability, and an obstacle to development and prosperity;
  - None of Iraq's communities will control the country through violence;
  - The United States respects the Iraqi people and does not seek dominance, exploitation,

or a long-term military presence;
- The United States does not favor one of Iraq's communities over the other but seeks to protect all of them and assure their participation in the political process;
- Supporting the Iraqi government and the Americans helps stabilize the country and entails rewards while supporting the insurgents entails costs and risks.
- To the insurgents and their supporters:
  - Violence will not work;
  - Abandoning the insurgency will bring personal and community rewards.
- To regional states:
  - Supporting the insurgents will entail political, economic and, potentially, military costs.
- To the global audience:
  - The Iraqi government is legitimate;
  - The insurgents are illegitimate—there are legitimate methods for the political inclusion and protection of the communities the insurgents claim to represent;
  - Every possible step is being taken to limit civilian casualties and sustain the rule of law;
  - The United States has no interest in dominating or exploiting Iraq, or sustaining a long-term military presence;
  - The conflict in Iraq is part of the global struggle against terrorism and extremism.

The military commander in-country had primary responsibility for communicating some of these messages, and played a supporting role in others. This will continue: strategic communications will always be a vital part of command during counterinsurgency.

RECOMMENDATIONS

U.S. military leaders cannot alter the basic dynamics of the American system for developing
strategy, or of the overarching strategic culture which
shapes the system. They must simply work within
them, remembering that military input into national
policy or grand strategy will always be valued or
ignored according to the proclivities of the President
and Secretary of Defense. If these political leaders want
to shut the military out, they will. Programs to increase
the number or the quality of strategic thinkers within
the Army—while they may be valuable—might not
affect the degree to which military advice influences
national policy and grand strategy. The limits on the
military role in crafting America's policy toward Iraq
during the Bush administration had little to do with
the quality of military advice and much to do with
the preferences and prejudices of President Bush and
Secretary Rumsfeld.

That said, the strategic shift of 2007 does suggest
a number of steps that the Army should undertake so
that it is prepared to play the most constructive role
and offer the best advice possible should the United
States once again consider or undertake involvement
in a large scale counterinsurgency campaign.

**Be skeptical of basing force development and
military strategy on the 2007-08 experience in Iraq.**
After the end of the Cold War, Operation DESERT
STORM became the paradigmatic conflict for force
development and planning. Whether labeled "major
theater war" (MTW) or "major combat operations"
(MCO), the thinking was that future wars would
look much like the one of 1990-91. Today Operation

IRAQI FREEDOM is becoming paradigmatic. Much of the force development and other change underway in the Army is driven by the desire to perform Iraq-like operations more effectively. This may be a classic case of the old problem of preparing to fight the *last* war. Most importantly, the strategic shift of 2007 — particularly the surge in forces — is being used as a model for the very different conflict in Afghanistan.[106] For instance, during a September 2008 interview Republican vice presidential candidate Sarah Palin said, "a surge in Afghanistan also will lead us to victory there as it has proven to have done in Iraq."[107] This myth is not limited to the former Alaska governor. At the operational level, commanders in Afghanistan have attempted to replicate the deployment of small American units into remote locations with the mission of population security. This worked in Iraq because the insurgents had already lost much of their local support, the population was weary of the conflict, and because support or reinforcement was close by. Afghanistan is different — none of these conditions apply.

To avoid this, the Army must recognize that the Iraq conflict in general, and the "perfect storm" of conditions contributing to the success of the strategic shift of 2007, will not be replicated. The two conflicts that the United States is using as models or para-digms — Iraq and Afghanistan — are actually outliers in the broader sweep of global conflict.[108] Both resulted from American intervention to remove hostile regimes. Iraq and Afghanistan were *destroyed* states, not *failed* states. In Iraq, the United States *created* the conditions for the insurgency. Hopefully this will not happen again. The Army should continue to mine Operation IRAQI FREEDOM and the strategic shift of 2007 for insights, but must be very wary when deriving general lessons from them or using them as the basis for force or strategy development.[109]

Use Army intellectual resources to lead a basic reconceptualization of the way that the joint community, the DoD, the other agencies of the U.S. Government, and American political leaders think about insurgency and counterinsurgency. The strategic shift of 2007 was necessary because in 2003, the Bush administration misunderstood the nature of the Iraqi political and economic system and destroyed that nation's parasitic state without a ready replacement, mistakenly believing that an effective and stable replacement would quickly emerge from the political rubble.[110] But the strategic shift was also necessary because once insurgency emerged in Iraq, the United States approached it with a flawed conceptualization. The Army had little control over the first misunderstanding. It could not have steered the administration from its chosen path of regime removal. But it could have helped the United States mitigate or avoid the second one with a more nuanced and sophisticated understanding of insurgency. To avoid a repetition of the disaster that Iraq had become by 2006, the Army should lead the joint community, the DoD, the other agencies of the U.S. Government, and American political leaders in a reconceptualization of insurgency and counterinsurgency.[111]

Since first embracing counterinsurgency during the Kennedy administration, the United States has considered it a form of war. That means that the goal is "victory" defined as the defeat of the enemy and decisive success. In the American view, insurgency emerges because of capability shortfalls by a government, be they political, economic, or security. Insurgents and the government then compete for the support of the population; the side that wins this competition will normally win the war. The American role is to augment the capability and legitimacy of the national government and help it directly defeat the insurgents and protect the population. This was never fully accurate. It reflected American perceptions and values as much as reality in the parts of the world where insurgency takes root.

As Iraq descended into sectarian violence and near chaos, the problem was not simply capability shortfalls. Government officials themselves were fueling sectarian violence. The Maliki regime was both part of the solution and part of the problem. Like most governments in the world (and nearly all of the ones vulnerable to insurgency), it operated by patronage and force. Like many of the states which seek American assistance, the Maliki regime made just enough reforms and controlled corruption and repression just enough to keep the aid flowing but rejected advice from Washington which might have challenged its hold on power. This was typical rather than abnormal. And Iraq did not reflect the American assumption that the people can be enticed into supporting the government rather than the insurgents by the provision of "goods," especially security, infrastructure improvements, political representation, and economic opportunity. As in most parts of the world, ties of affinity — religion, sect, ethnicity, tribe, clan, race, and so forth — mattered as much or more than which side in the conflict was likely to provide the most goods. Outside Baghdad, Iraq's Sunni Arabs did not shift their allegiance from insurgents to the government because of American efforts. The insurgency split and those insurgents who changed sides brought their supporters with them.

So the American image of insurgency clashed mightily with reality. Eventually, the military and the U.S. embassy adjusted to reality and crafted a strategy that only partly reflected the American conceptualization of insurgency (and doctrine, which is its codification). This worked both because of the talent of the U.S. military and civilian leaders, and because the lucky confluence of trends provided a window of opportunity. The next time America may not be so lucky. This suggests that we need a more accurate and nuanced conceptualization of insurgency based on the reality of identity, affinity, and governance in those regions of the world where insurgency occurs. It must recognize that in some instances, the people simply cannot be convinced to support the government. Population-centric counterinsurgency, as Gian Gentile argues, is an operational method which may apply in some settings, but is not a strategy independent of culture and policy objectives.[112] A new conceptualization of insurgency must recognize that corrupt governments which lack control of much of their own territory are the norm in much of the world. It must also recognize that subnational organizations are more politically, economically, and militarily important than the national government in much of the world. The Army, with its massive analytical, intellectual, and war-gaming capability, is the organization best equipped to lead this reconceptualization. The Training and Doctrine Command (TRADOC), in close conjunction with the Joint Forces Command, must be the primary driver of this process.

Increase attention to strategic communication skills in leader selection and development programs. Declining public and congressional support for American engagement in Iraq forced the Bush administration to accept increased operational risk lest its mandate to remain engaged crumble before the Iraqi security forces were self-sustaining. In this case, the United States did not pay a strategic price for this, but might in the future. Hence sustaining public and congressional support for engagement in protracted counterinsurgency, stability operations, or peacekeeping is vital. Clearly the President and other top civilian policymakers will bear the brunt of the responsibility for this but because the U.S. military commander will be seen as the face of the American effort, he too must contribute to the effort. Phrased differently, "strategic communications" will be a particularly vital skill for the commander of a counterinsurgency campaign. The commander of a large scale counterinsurgency campaign without the requisite personal skill set will be vulnerable to failure and replacement. So if counterinsurgency is to remain a central element of American strategy — and it currently appears that it will — the Army should refine and improve its existing procedures for helping future commanders with strategic communications.[113] The promotion system should reflect the importance of this skill.

Develop a rapidly deployable surge capacity for creating, training, and equipping local security forces. Training and advising local allies will remain the key to counterinsurgency support, but it is crucial for the United States to be able to do this quickly in failed or destroyed states before an insurgency can coalesce. History suggests that insurgencies always need a breathing space to organize and begin operations. The government may be unaware of them or simply lack the capability to quash them before they evolve from proto-insurgencies to full blown ones.[114] As David Gompert and John Gordon noted, "Proto-insurgents may be barely noticeable, not seen as having the potential to inspire insurgency, or dismissed as criminals or inconsequential crack-pots."[115] Until a government recognizes the existence and extent of an insurgency, it cannot act.

Stopping an insurgency from developing involves both recognition and action. In Iraq, recognition took several months. Insurgency only takes root when a government or ruling authority has failed in major ways. In Iraq the Bush administration, particularly Secretary Rumsfeld, were loath to admit the short-comings of the Coalition Provisional Authority and denied that an insurgency existed long after it was perfectly clear. Even as late as 2005, Rumsfeld claimed there was no organized insurgency and instructed the DoD to avoid using that word.[116] As Bradley Graham explained,

> For Rumsfeld to have concurred that an insurgency had taken root in Iraq would have led him to acknowledge the enemy as an organized and durable force. That, in turn, would have pointed to a much longer struggle ahead for U.S. forces, since historically insurgencies were not quickly defeated.[117]

With recognition delayed, it took several years for the United States to develop an effective organization and system for training and advising the ISF. Had this been done in the summer and autumn of 2003, there is a good chance the insurgency would never have taken root. While the Army will never be able to force policymakers to recognize the emergence of an insurgency and commit the United States to action against it, Army leaders can be prepared to act quickly once a decision is made. To do this, the U.S. military should be able to deploy a major training and advisory effort on short notice, seizing the "golden moment" before the insurgency matures. The first U.S. trainers and advisers in a security force assistance surge should be deployed within weeks of warning, with a contingent on the ground as soon as possible.[118] Having a major training and advisory capability ready to deploy in weeks or months rather than developing it over several years would require major changes in the Army and significant ones in the other services. In all likelihood, it would require a refocusing of a significant portion of the Reserve Component on this mission, the creation of at least a small standing advisory corps within the active Army, and the development of methods to hire and deploy contractors much more rapidly than was possible during the early years of the Iraq conflict. It might also be possible for the combatant commands to create regional stability support centers and hold large scale multinational exercises to make it easier to surge a multinational training and advisory force to forestall an insurgency in a failed or destroyed state.

Maintain the Army's wartime adaptation speed. The strategic surge of 2007 was possible because the U.S. military had developed the ability to adapt rapidly as insurgent tactics and operational methods shifted. The lessons learned process had become very powerful not only in its ability to collect relevant information, but also its ability to integrate that information into training and education, disseminate it within the services, and use it for doctrine development and the fielding of new equipment and technology. Informal learning, much of it based on information technology, supported the process. Speeding the adaptation process during war is normal. By the end of the world wars, for instance, changes in methods, organization, technology, and equipment—which would have taken years or decades during peacetime—were unfolding in weeks or months. It is important that the Army not allow this speed of adaptation to devolve back into a normal peacetime pace once the conflict in Iraq (and Afghanistan) ends. Army leaders must institutionalize it lest it again take several years to recreate it during future conflicts. Finding the best method of this will require significant analysis and experimentation — something that should begin immediately.

Lead an effort within the joint community to develop and institutionalize procedures for reseizing the strategic initiative. In 2003, the United States had the strategic initiative in Iraq. By 2006, it was lost. The insurgents controlled the evolution of the conflict. This should have been expected, since what is called the "paradoxical logic of strategy" explains, every strategy eventually loses effectiveness if not altered.[119] But in 2007, the United States was able to reseize the strategic initiative by the top down initiative of the surge and the bottom up initiative of collaborating with Sunni Arab militias. The effort, imagination, and talent of many military and civilian leaders and national security experts allowed this. It was not something they were educated to do. For decades, American military leaders had studied and wargamed conflicts in which the enemy initially seized the strategic initiative through aggression. But once the United States struck back, it held the strategic initiative until the end of the conflict. This was the way a war with the Soviet bloc was conceptualized, and the way that Operation DESERT STORM unfolded. So American leaders had not thought through the complexities of a protracted conflict in which the enemy had been able to wrest the strategic initiative from the United States.

Luckily, American leaders were able to figure out how to regain the strategic initiative. But we should not leave our future to luck. We should abandon the assumption that in all conflicts, once the United States gains the strategic initiative it will hold it to the end of the conflict. The U.S. military should use historical research and wargames to understand the mechanics of reseizing the strategic initiative in a conflict, seeking to find what works and what does not. The military may *hope* for short conflicts where the strategic initiative does not change hands but should not *assume* them. Once a body of theory and concepts on this topic are developed, the military should integrate them into its professional educational system and articulate them to civilian policymakers who, in nearly all cases, will not have learned strategy in a formal setting such as the war colleges.

CONCLUSION

The strategic shift of 2007 in Iraq shows both the strengths of the American strategy making system and the U.S. military, and some of their enduring problems, particularly in protracted counterinsurgency support. It demonstrates that the process for integrating professional military advice into strategy making is imperfect, and that solutions are difficult and largely beyond the control of the military itself. To the extent that military advice was ineffective during the reassessment of American strategy that took place in the second half of 2006, it was not because of a lack of talent or expertise. Rather it was the nature of the American system that muted the military's input. Counterinsurgency, which is protracted, ambiguous, and quintessentially psychological, compounded the problems.

The events also demonstrated that the process of *institutionalizing* a strategic decision—of convincing key stakeholders, the Congress, and the public — is as important as actually arriving at a decision. Most of what became the strategic shift of 2007 was developed by a small group of people in the White House and NSC between September 2006 and early December of that year. But only when President Bush, assisted by the AEI's study and other factors, was able to convince key stakeholders in the DoD, the Congress, and the public was the decision implementable or real.

The Army learned much in Iraq and has taken great strides to integrate the lessons. Much work, though, remains to be done. Finally, enduring solutions can only come about if Congress and the President understand what went wrong in Iraq between 2003 and 2007, and realize that something like it could happen again. The United States was fortunate in Iraq. To some extent, America must always depend on luck. But it can, through preparation, lessen this dependence.

ENDNOTES

1. Condoleezza Rice, interview with Al-Arabiya Television Network, December 2, 2006.

2. This section draws heavily from Steven Metz, *Iraq and the Evolution of American Strategy*, Washington, DC: Potomac, 2008; and *idem, Learning From Iraq: Counterinsurgency and American Strategy*, Carlisle Barracks, PA: Strategic Studies Institute, U.S. Army War College, 2006.

3. There are conflicting accounts of who fired first. See Ian Fisher, "U.S. Force Said To Kill 15 Iraqis During an Anti-American Rally," *New York Times*, April 30, 2003.

4. Donald H. Rumsfeld, Prepared Testimony for the Senate Armed Services Committee, Washington, DC, July 9, 2003.

5. "DoD News Briefing — Mr. Di Rita and General Abizaid," U.S. Department of Defense news transcript, July 16, 2003. See

also Vernon Loeb, "'Guerrilla' War Acknowledged," *Washington Post*, July 17, 2003; and David Cloud and Greg Jaffe, *The Fourth Star: Four Generals and the Epic Struggle For the Future of the United States Army*, New York: Crown, 2009, pp. 127-128.

6. A government facing an insurgency undertakes counterinsurgency. Outsiders like the United States provide counterinsurgency support.

7. Linda Robinson, *Tell Me How This Ends: General David Petraeus and the Search For a Way Out of Iraq*, New York: Public Affairs, 2008, p. 14.

8. *Measuring Stability and Security in Iraq: Report to Congress in Accordance With the Department of Defense Appropriations Act 2007*, November 2006, p. 17.

9. *Measuring Stability and Security in Iraq: Report to Congress in Accordance With the Department of Defense Appropriations Act 2007*, March 2009, p. 19.

10. "Victory in Iraq," *New York Sun*, July 18, 2008. Other examples of the same idea are Jeff Jacoby, "Bush's 'Folly' Is Ending in Victory," *Boston Globe*, March 25, 2009; and, "Quiet Victory in Iraq," *National Review*, February 2, 2009. The online edition of the *Weekly Standard*, which was always at the forefront of advocacy for American involvement in Iraq, stated that "Obama has inherited victory in Iraq" (available from *weeklystandard.com*, posting by Michael Goldfarb, January 20, 2009). Rush Limbaugh referred to "the surge that led to victory in Iraq" (e.g., transcript of July 1, 2009 broadcast.) Speaking on Fox News on February 15, 2009, commentator Oliver North opined, "Today, the campaign against radical Islam in Iraq is won."

11. This stress on the symbolic content of security issues is a characteristic of dominant powers. All of history's great states and empires recognized that other nations drew cues from the way they interacted with enemies and allies. Lesser powers, which play a smaller role in determining the rules of behavior for regional or global security systems, are less concerned with the symbolism of their actions and more with the tangible outcomes.

12. *National Strategy for Victory in Iraq*, Washington, DC: National Security Council, 2005, p. 1.

13. "Press Conference by the President," Washington, DC, August 21, 2006.

14. This reflected an intellectual tradition that can be traced back to the philosophy of history developed by Georg Wilhelm Friedrich Hegel and codified in Ronald Reagan's thinking. In *Iraq and the Evolution of American Strategy*, I argue that President Bush was driven by a desire to emulate Reagan. This made him receptive to the Reaganesque portrayal of history as a great struggle between freedom and its enemies, and the United States as the champion of freedom.

15. "President's Address to the Nation," Washington, DC, September 11, 2006. This assertion was never seriously questioned, demonstrating the degree to which the 9/11 attacks had skewed American thinking about security and made any assertion about terrorism credible.

16. Peter D. Feaver, "Anatomy of the Surge," *Commentary*, April 2008, p. 25.

17. Letter to President Bush signed by Harry Reid, Nancy Pelosi, Dick Durbin, Steny Hoyer, Carl Levin, Ike Skelton, Joe Biden, Tom Lantos, Jay Rockefeller, Jane Harmon, Daniel Inouye, and John Murtha, July 31, 2006.

18. Robin Toner and Jim Rutenberg, "Partisan Divide on Iraq Exceeds Split on Vietnam," *New York Times*, July 30, 2006, p. 1.

19. Jeffrey M. Jones, "Bush Quarterly Average Establishes New Low: 29%," *Gallup Report*, July 17, 2008.

20. Adam Nagourney, Jim Rutenberg, and Jeff Zeleny, "Democrats Turned War Into an Ally," *New York Times*, November 9, 2006, p. A1.

21. Quoted in Michael Grunwald, "Opposition to War Buoys Democrats," *Washington Post*, November 8, 2006, p. A31.

22. David S. Cloud, "Senator Says U.S. Should Rethink Iraq Strategy," *New York Times*, October 6, 2006, p. A12.

23. Chuck Hagel, "Leaving Iraq, Honorably," *Washington Post*, November 26, 2006, p. B7.

24. "Rumsfeld's Memo of Options for Iraq War," reprinted in the *New York Times*, December 3, 2006.

25. Robin Wright, "Bush Initiates Iraq Policy Review Separate From Baker Group's," *Washington Post*, November 15, 2006, p. A16.

26. See Steven Metz, "America's Defense Transformation: A Conceptual and Political History," *Defence Studies*, Vol. 6, No. 1, March 2006, pp. 1-25; and Frederick W. Kagan, *Finding the Target: The Transformation of American Military Policy*, New York: Encounter, 2006.

27. *An Analysis of the U.S. Military's Ability to Sustain an Occupation of Iraq*, Washington, DC: Congressional Budget Office, September 3, 2003.

28. The most comprehensive treatment of this was Thomas Donnelly and Frederic W. Kagan, *Ground Truth: The Future of U.S. Land Power*, Washington, DC: American Enterprise Institute, 2008.

29. Michael O'Hanlon of the Brookings Institution and Frederick Kagan of the American Enterprise Institute have been among the most persistent in calling for an increase in the size of the Army. See, for instance, O'Hanlon's "Breaking the Army," *Washington Post*, July 3, 2003; "The Need to Increase the Size of the Deployable Army," *Parameters*, Vol. 34, No. 3, Autumn 2004, pp. 4-17; and *Defense Policy for the Post-Saddam Era*, Washington, DC: Brookings Institution, 2005; and Kagan's "The Army We Have: It's Too Small," *Weekly Standard*, December 27, 2004; "Army Needs More Strength in Numbers," *New York Daily News*, August 24, 2006; and "The U.S. Military's Manpower Crisis," *Foreign Affairs*, Vol. 85, No. 4, July/August 2006, pp. 97-110. Other organizations and individuals took a similar line. In January 2005, for instance, the Project for the New American Century sent a letter to leading members of Congress. The letter included a call for increasing the

number of U.S. ground forces. The signatories included defense experts from both ends of the political spectrum, retired senior military leaders, and former officials of the Clinton and George H. W. Bush administrations.

30. Mark Sappenfield, "Dueling Views on Army Size: Congress vs. Rumsfeld," *Christian Science Monitor*, May 17, 2005. In early 2004, a bipartisan group of 128 members of the House, led by Heather Wilson (R-NM), called on President Bush to increase the Army's overall size—called end strength—and to reduce the time reservists must spend on active duty. In October 2004, the FY 2005 Defense Authorization Act increased Army end strength by 20,000 and Marine Corps end strength by 3,000 with additional increases authorized in future years. For background, see Edward F. Bruner, *Military Forces: What Is the Appropriate Size for the United States?* Congressional Research Service Report for Congress, May 28, 2004. The National Defense Authorization Act for Fiscal Year 2006 (Public Law 109-163) authorized an active duty end strength for the Army at 512,400 and 179,000 for the Marine Corps. Additional authority also was provided in section 403 of that Act to increase the active duty end strength for the Army by up to 20,000 and Marine Corps active duty end strength by 5,000 during fiscal years 2007 through 2009.

31. Donald H. Rumsfeld, "New Model Army," *Wall Street Journal*, February 3, 2004.

32. Esther Schrader, "Army Says It Has Enough Troops For Three More Years," *Los Angeles Times*, June 16, 2004.

33. Quoted in Ann Scott Tyson, "Two Years Later, Iraq War Drains Military," *Washington Post*, March 19, 2005.

34. For instance, see James Fallows, "The Hollow Army," *Atlantic*, March 2004, pp. 29-31.

35. Ann Scott Tyson, "General Says Army Will Need to Grow," *Washington Post*, December 15, 2006, p. A1.

36. Thom Shanker, "Joint Chiefs Chairman Looks Beyond Current Wars," *New York Times*, October 22, 2007.

37. See Bob Woodward, *State of Denial*, New York: Simon and

Schuster, 2006, pp. 440-491; Kimberly Kagan, *The Surge: A Military History*, New York: Encounter, 2009, pp. 3-26; and Bing West, *The Strongest Tribe: War, Politics, and the Endgame in Iraq*, New York: Random House, 2008, pp. 64-172.

38. Bob Woodward, *The War Within: A Secret White House History 2006-2008*, New York: Simon and Schuster, 2008, p. 7.

39. West, p. 198.

40. Cloud and Jaffe, p. 169.

41. West, pp. 164-165; Kagan, *The Surge*, pp. 11-15; and, Catherine Dale, *Operation Iraqi Freedom: Strategies, Approaches, Results, and Issues for Congress*, Washington, DC: Congressional Research Service, 2009, pp. 69-70. Then-Major General James Thurman, commander of the Multi-National Division-Baghdad, described Operation TOGETHER FORWARD as "an Iraqi-led operation . . . to reduce the sectarian violence in focused areas identified by the Iraqi government" and with a strategy of three parts: clear, hold, and build. (DoD News Briefing with Major General Thurman from Iraq, September 22, 2006).

42. Information technology and the profusion of media have exacerbated this since the public now sees American troops as individuals rather than simply statistics.

43. Kagan, *The Surge*, p. 32.

44. Hadley's pessimistic memo was quickly leaked and reprinted in several media sources.

45. Bob Woodward, "CIA Said Instability Seemed 'Irreversible'," *Washington Post*, July 12, 2007. A CIA spokesman later disputed Woodward's account but other sources confirmed it. The testimony itself was never made public.

46. West, p. 198.

47. Woodward, *The War Within*, p. 22; Bradley Graham, *By His*

Own Rules: The Ambitions, Successes, and Ultimate Failures of Donald Rumsfeld, New York: PublicAffairs, 2009, pp. 624-625.

48. West, p. 160.

49. Woodward, *The War Within*, p. 170.

50. West, pp. 217-218.

51. Robinson, p. 36.

52. President's Address to the Nation, January 10, 2007.

53. Kalev I. Sepp, "Best Practices in Counterinsurgency," *Military Review*, Vol. 85, No. 3, May-June 2005, pp. 8-12. From 2007 to 2009, Sepp served in the Office of the Secretary of Defense as a Deputy Assistant Secretary for Special Operations Capabilities.

54. Bruce Hoffman, *Insurgency and Counterinsurgency in Iraq*, Santa Monica, CA: RAND Corporation, 2004.

55. John A. Nagl, *Learning to Eat Soup with a Knife: Counterinsurgency Lessons from Malaya and Vietnam*, Chicago: University of Chicago Press, 2005; and David Kilcullen, "Counterinsurgency Redux," *Survival*, Vol. 48, No. 4, Winter 2006-07, pp. 111-130. Both Nagl and Kilcullen were also Ph.D.s.

56. Andrew F. Krepinevich, Jr., "How to Win in Iraq," *Foreign Affairs*, Vol. 84, No. 5, September-October 2005, pp. 87-91.

57. See *Report of the National Defense Panel*, Arlington, VA: National Defense Panel, 1997.

58. Andrew F. Krepinevich, Jr., *The Army and Vietnam*, Baltimore, MD: Johns Hopkins University Press, 1986.

59. Krepinevich, "How to Win in Iraq," pp. 88-89 .

60. Steven N. Simon, *After the Surge: The Case for U.S. Disengagement From Iraq*, New York: Council on Foreign Relations, February 2007; *idem*, "America and Iraq: The Case for Disengagement," *Survival*, Vol. 49, No. 1, Spring 2007, pp. 61-84;

and Lawrence J. Korb and Max A. Bergmann, "How to Withdraw Quickly and Safely," *Boston Globe*, September 9, 2007. Also see Rosa Brooks, "Abandon Iraq to Save It," *Los Angeles Times*, December 1, 2006, p. A35 .

61. Zbigniew Brzezinski, "It Is Time to Plan for an American Withdrawal From Iraq," *Financial Times*, April 19, 2006, p. 15; and William E. Odom, "Cut and Run? You Bet," *Foreign Policy*, Vol. 154, May/June 2006, pp. 60-61.

62. The Iraq Study Group was chaired by James Baker, George H.W. Bush's Secretary of State; and former Democratic Congressman Lee Hamilton. Its members included former Supreme Court Justice Sandra Day O'Connor, former Secretary of State Lawrence Eagleburger, former Attorney General Edwin Meese III, former Republican Senator Alan K. Simpson, business executive Vernon Jordan, Jr., former White House Chief of Staff (and current CIA Director) Leon E. Panetta, former Secretary of Defense William J. Perry, and former Democratic governor and Senator Charles S. Robb.

63. See *The Iraq Study Group Report*, December 2, 2006, pp. 32-62.

64. Robinson, p. 32; Woodward, *The War Within*, pp. 131-132; and Graham, pp. 636-640.

65. West, p. 218; Robinson, p. 33.

66. Frederick W. Kagan, *Choosing Victory: A Plan for Success in Iraq*, Phase I Report of the American Enterprise Institute Iraq Planning Group, n.d., p. 5. The AEI Group included Frederick W. Kagan, Jack Keane, David Barno, Danielle Pletka, Rend al-Rahim, Joel Armstrong, Daniel Dwyer, Larry Crandall, Larry Sampler, Michael Eisenstadt, Kimberly Kagan, Michael Rubin, Reuel Marc Gerecht, Thomas Donnelly, Gary Schmitt, Mauro De Lorenzo, and Vance Serchuk.

67. *Field Manual (FM) 3-24/Marine Corps Warfighting Publication (MCWP) 3-33.5, Counterinsurgency*, Washington, DC: Headquarters, Department of the Army, December 2006, p. 1-23.

68. See, for instance, David S. Cloud, "Senator Says U.S.

Should Rethink Iraq Strategy," *New York Times*, October 6, 2006, p. A12; and Chuck Hagel, "Leaving Iraq, Honorably," *Washington Post*, November 26, 2006, p. B7.

69. See Metz, *Iraq and the Evolution of American Strategy*, pp. 101-138; and Barton Gellman, *Angler: The Cheney Vice Presidency*, New York: Penguin, 2008, pp. 131-253.

70. Gellman contends that Cheney's influence was waning by 2006.

71. Woodward, *The War Within*, p. 20.

72. Secretary of State Condoleezza Rice, "Iraq and U.S. Policy," testimony to the Senate Committee on Foreign Relations, October 19, 2005.

73. Woodward, *The War Within*, pp. 31-33. While Woodward had extensive access to key administration officials, no other source to date has independently verified his depiction of this process.

74. Title 10 U.S. Code, Chap. 5, § 151 states:

(b) Function as Military Advisers. —
   (1) The Chairman of the Joint Chiefs of Staff is the principal military adviser to the President, the National Security Council, the Homeland Security Council, and the Secretary of Defense.
   (2) The other members of the Joint Chiefs of Staff are military advisers to the President, the National Security Council, the Homeland Security Council, and the Secretary of Defense as specified in subsections (d) and (e).

(c) Consultation by Chairman. —
   (1) In carrying out his functions, duties, and responsibilities, the Chairman shall, as he considers appropriate, consult with and seek the advice of —
      (A) the other members of the Joint Chiefs of Staff; and
      (B) the commanders of the unified and specified combatant commands.

(2) Subject to subsection (d), in presenting advice with respect to any matter to the President, the National Security Council, the Homeland Security Council, or the Secretary of Defense, the Chairman shall, as he considers appropriate, inform the President, the National Security Council, the Homeland Security Council, or the Secretary of Defense, as the case may be, of the range of military advice and opinion with respect to that matter.

(d) Advice and Opinions of Members Other Than Chairman. —
 (1) A member of the Joint Chiefs of Staff (other than the Chairman) may submit to the Chairman advice or an opinion in disagreement with, or advice or an opinion in addition to, the advice presented by the Chairman to the President, the National Security Council, the Homeland Security Council, or the Secretary of Defense. If a member submits such advice or opinion, the Chairman shall present the advice or opinion of such member at the same time he presents his own advice to the President, the National Security Council, the Homeland Security Council, or the Secretary of Defense, as the case may be.
 (2) The Chairman shall establish procedures to ensure that the presentation of his own advice to the President, the National Security Council, the Homeland Security Council, or the Secretary of Defense is not unduly delayed by reason of the submission of the individual advice or opinion of another member of the Joint Chiefs of Staff.

(e) Advice on Request. — The members of the Joint Chiefs of Staff, individually or collectively, in their capacity as military advisers, shall provide advice to the President, the National Security Council, the Homeland Security Council, or the Secretary of Defense on a particular matter when the President, the National Security Council, the Homeland Security Council, or the Secretary requests such advice.

75. *National Strategy for Victory in Iraq*, Washington, DC: National Security Council, 2005, p. 1.

76. West, p. 217.

77. *Ibid.*, p. 204.

78. General Casey also believed Maliki could be an effective national leader. See Cloud and Jaffe, p. 253.

79. Woodward, *The War Within*, pp. 190-92.

80. West, p. 202.

81. For instance, General Abizaid continued to warn that the American military was stretched too thin to sustain a long-term troop increase in Iraq. See Michael R. Gordon and Mark Mazzetti, "General Warns of Risks in Iraq if G.I.'s are Cut," *New York Times*, November 16, 2006, p. A1.

82. Woodward, *The War Within*, pp. 232-233.

83. *Ibid.*, p. 238.

84. This is a persistent problem in counterinsurgency support. It was also evident in Vietnam and today has reappeared in Afghanistan.

85. See, for instance, General Abizaid's testimony to the Senate Armed Services Committee, November 15, 2006.

86. *The Iraq Study Group Report*, p. 48.

87. It was actually more a refinement of the existing strategy than a new one.

88. David Kilcullen, *The Accidental Guerrilla: Fighting Small Wars in the Midst of a Big One*, Oxford, UK: Oxford University Press, 2009, pp. 133-135.

89. Cloud and Jaffe, pp. 264-265.

90. See Austin Long, "The Anbar Awakening," *Survival*, Vol. 50, No. 2, April-May 2008, pp. 67-94.

91. Robinson, p. 106. Of course, the full story of the high value targeting campaign will not be publicly available for many years. For conceptual treatments of high value targeting and counterinsurgency/counterterrorism, see George A. Crawford,

Manhunting: Reversing the Polarity of Warfare, Baltimore, MD: PublishAmerica, 2008; *idem, Manhunting: Counter-Network Organization for Irregular Warfare*, Hurlburt Field, FL: Joint Special Operations University Press, 2009; and Steven Metz, "Strategic Decapitation: The Dynamics of High Value Targeting in Counterinsurgency," paper prepared for the RAND Corporation Insurgency Board, July 2008.

92. The notion of victory pushed by some on the political right may be premature, the possibility of renewed civil war and disintegration remain as the American role—and ability to influence events—diminishes. See, for instance, Ernest Londono and Greg Jaffe, "Iraq Carnage Shows Sectarian War Goes On," *Washington Post*, August 20, 2009. Iraq may eventually face what might be called a "resurgency"—an insurgency that appears defeated or goes into hibernation and later reappears if the root causes are not addressed.

93. See FM 3-24/MCWP 3-33.5, December 2006; and *U.S. Government Counterinsurgency Guide*, Washington, DC: U.S. Department of State Bureau of Political-Military Affairs, 2009.

94. West, p. 223.

95. Cloud and Jaffe recount Maliki's congratulations to General Petraeus after his September 2007 congressional testimony, suggesting that the Iraqi leader was well aware of the importance of support for his regime in Washington. See Cloud and Jaffe, p. 277.

96. British Lieutenant General (Ret.) Graeme Lamb makes this same point in Dexter Filkins, "Stanley McChrystal's Long War," *New York Times Magazine*, October 18, 2009.

97. See James Kitfield, *War and Destiny: How the Bush Revolution in Foreign and Military Affairs Redefined American Power*, Washington, DC: Potomac, 2005; Dale R. Herspring, *Rumsfeld's Wars: The Arrogance of Power*, Lawrence: University Press of Kansas, 2008; and Charles A. Stevenson, *SECDEF: The Nearly Impossible Job of Secretary of Defense*, Washington, DC: Potomac, 2006, pp. 159-180. Bradley Graham cites former Undersecretary of Defense for Policy Eric Edelman as indicating that Rumsfeld tended to be

more deferential to the regional combatant commanders than the Service chiefs or Joint Staff. See pp. 641-642.

98. Cloud and Jaffe, p. 171.

99. For instance, Myers's memoirs make no mention of direct, private conversations with the President. See Richard B. Myers, *Eyes on the Horizon: Serving on the Front Lines of National Security*, New York: Threshold, 2009. In *State of Denial* and *The War Within*, Bob Woodward describes a few meetings between General Pace and President Bush but does not suggest that these were decisive or even important in shaping the administration's Iraq policy.

100. Vice President Cheney, though, did reach down into the bureaucracy and deal directly with second tier officials. See Gellman, p. 196.

101. H.R. McMaster, *Dereliction of Duty: Lyndon Johnson, Robert McNamara, the Joint Chiefs of Staff, and the Lies that Led to Vietnam*, New York: HarperCollins, 1997, pp. 328-329. Like John Nagl's *Counterinsurgency Lessons from Malaya and Vietnam* and Andrew Krepinevich's *The Army and Vietnam*, McMaster's book began as a Ph.D. dissertation while he was serving on the faculty of the U.S. Military Academy.

102. In describing the role of CENTCOM commander General Tommy Franks during the planning for the 2003 invasion of Iraq, Thomas Ricks entitled a section of his book *Fiasco*, "Franks Flunks Strategy." This was not an isolated phenomenon.

103. Another example of important innovation emerging from the "upper middle" level is the role that Douglas Macgregor's *Breaking the Phalanx: A New Design for Landpower in the 21st Century*, New York: Praeger, 1997, played in helping the Army move to a brigade-based organization.

104. Quoted in Woodward, *The War Within*, p. 197.

105. General Casey's tour in Iraq was extended three times to allow this. See Cloud and Jaffe, p. 193.

106. See, for instance, Frederick W. Kagan and Kimberley Kagan, "In Afghanistan, Real Leverage Starts With More Troops," *Washington Post*, November 27, 2009. Following President Obama's December 1, 2009, speech on Afghanistan at the U.S. Military Academy, Senator Joe Lieberman said he was encouraged by the announcement of a troop increase because, "It's the strategy that worked in Iraq." Quoted in Susan Page and Kathy Kiely, "Dems Balk at Deployment Plan," *USA Today*, December 2, 2009. For an assessment of using Iraq as a model for Afghanistan, see Charles D. Allen, "The Danger of Déjà Vu: Why the Iraq Surge Is Not a Lesson for Afghanistan," *Armed Forces Journal*, December 2009/January 2010, pp. 30-41.

107. Sarah Palin, interviewed by Katie Couric on CBS News, September 24, 2008.

108. This observation was inspired by comments by Mary Kaldor of the London School of Economics at a September 2009 conference at the U.S. Naval War College.

109. It might be possible to use the Iraq conflict as a model for *leader* development since this is less context-dependent than force or strategy development.

110. See Jeffrey Record, *Wanting War: Why the Bush Administration Invaded Iraq*, Washington, DC: Potomac, 2009.

111. This section builds on Steven Metz, *Rethinking Insurgency*, Carlisle, PA: Strategic Studies Institute, U.S. Army War College, 2007.

112. Gian P. Gentile, "A Strategy of Tactics: Population-centric COIN and the Army," *Parameters*, Vol. 39, No. 3, Autumn 2009, pp. 5-17.

113. While dealing with combatant commanders rather than commanders of counterinsurgency efforts specifically, there is excellent analysis in Jeffrey B. Jones, Daniel T. Kuehl, Daniel Burgess, and Russell Rochte, "Strategic Communication and the Combatant Commander," *Joint Force Quarterly*, Vol 55, 4th Quarter, 2009, pp. 104-108.

114. On this concept, see Daniel Byman, *Understanding Proto-Insurgencies*, Santa Monica, CA: RAND Corporation, 2007.

115. David C. Gompert and John Gordon IV, *War by Other Means: Building Complete and Balanced Capabilities for Counterinsurgency*, Santa Monica, CA: RAND Corporation, 2008, p. 36.

116. Dana Milbank, "Rumsfeld's War on 'Insurgents'," *Washington Post*, November 30, 2005. General (Ret.) Jack Keane told *Washington Post* reporter Bradley Graham that when he sensed the beginning of an insurgency in the summer of 2003, General Myers advised him to avoid such talk with Rumsfeld. See Graham, p. 424.

117. Graham, p. 427.

118. Gompert and Gordon suggest "early," "medium," "late," and "never" capabilities that U.S. advisers and trainers should impart to partner states fighting an insurgency (*War by Other Means*, pp. 209-210). Whether their particular construct is the correct one, clearly some capabilities must take priority.

119. See Edward Luttwak, *Strategy: The Logic of War and Peace*, Cambridge, MA: Belknap, 1987.

U.S. ARMY WAR COLLEGE

Major General Robert M. Williams
Commandant

*****

STRATEGIC STUDIES INSTITUTE

Director
Professor Douglas C. Lovelace, Jr.

Director of Research
Dr. Antulio J. Echevarria II

Author
Dr. Steven Metz

Executive Editor
Colonel John R. Martin, U.S. Army (Retired)

Director of Publications
Dr. James G. Pierce

Publications Assistant
Ms. Rita A. Rummel

*****

Composition
Mrs. Jennifer E. Nevil

www.ingramcontent.com/pod-product-compliance
Lightning Source LLC
Chambersburg PA
CBHW080208300326
41934CB00039B/3413